NFHS Baseball Rules

in

Black and White

2019 – 2020

Jim Bettencourt

BLUE RIVER PRESS

Indianapolis, Indiana

NFHS Baseball Rules in Black and White 2019 – 2020

Published by Blue River Press
Indianapolis, Indiana
www.brpressbooks.com

Distributed by Cardinal Publishers Group
A Tom Doherty Company, Inc.
www.cardinalpub.com

ISBN 978-1-68157-152-2

Cover Design: Scott Lohr
Book Design: Dave Reed
Cover Photo: Dreamstime
Editor: Dani McCormick

Printed in the United States of America

10 9 8 7 6 5 4 3 2 1   19 20 21 22 23 24 25 26 27 28

Dedication

This book is dedicated to thousands of incredibly committed and hard-working men and women umpires who are always striving to improve their profession in order to make the game of baseball even better.

Contents

Foreword

As the Executive Instructional Chairman, California Baseball Umpires I am well aware of the challenges umpires face every season simply interpreting the rules of baseball. These challenges of the baseball rule book can reduce an umpire's ability to clearly retain and correctly call a ruling during a game. This is especially true for newer umpires, but also impacts veteran umpires.

I have waited years for an enhanced version of the high school rule book to become available to address these challenges and now, *Baseball Rules in Black and White* is here! Gone are the days of randomly searching for a rule, just to find arbitrary rule language. Or have the rule book direct me to three additional rules that are possibly related, or not in two other sections of the rule book.

It is my opinion *NFHS Baseball Rules in Black and White: 2019 – 2020* reader friendly content and format should be read and studied by every high school umpire and coach across the country. I will definitely have a copy on hand to quickly assist me with rule interpretations this high school season.

With *Baseball Rules in Black and White* you are able to quickly find a rule that has been converted into accurate Basic English, plus rule and page numbers from the official rule book are included. Best of all, rulings include related rulings that apply, all together on the same page. In addition, there are examples, exceptions, and author's notes all in large font.

I'm positive, the *NFHS Baseball Rules in Black and White: 2019 – 2020* can effectively increase your ability to clearly understand and retain what you have read. Even better, as an umpire you will have a much greater chance to confidently apply the entire correct ruling during a game.

—Bradley Hungerford, Executive Instructional Chairman
of the California Baseball Umpires Association

Introduction

Why do some umpires make confusing and arbitrary rulings during a baseball game?

It's not because umpires are blind, stupid, fat, skinny, slow, fast, tall, short, hard-nosed, or jokers. It's not because the umpire hates your team or favors the other team. It's not because he wants to get home early or stay away from his home longer. No, none of these reasons apply to why umpires make confusing and arbitrary rulings during a baseball game.

The real reason some umpires make confusing and arbitrary rulings during a baseball game, it is because the rule book itself is confusing and arbitrary. Rule book language is poorly written, making it extremely difficult to understand, retain, and apply when needed.

A large percentage of coaches and players seldom open a rule book. Not because they know all the rules, but because they despise the rule book language and format. This also explains a very good reason why so many coaches, players, and fans feel they can challenge an umpire's ruling, because they know just how confusing the baseball rule book language and format is.

So, with all this said, how do umpires like the baseball rule book?

Umpires usually fall into two camps on this topic, ones who believe the rule book is just fine as is and those who believe there has to be a better way.

The first smaller camp of umpires will claim the current rule book language and format is satisfactory. Most have come to this conclusion through a learn-as-you-go approach, during their time of umpiring. What's wrong with this philosophy? Learning (by mistake) along the way.

The second camp of umpires will come right out and tell you how absurd and challenging the baseball rule book's language and format are. This is particularly true with newer officials, but it is also true with many experienced umpires as well.

One area all umpires will agree is that they all want to get the call right. Even though at times it may not appear that way, umpires really do want the correct call made. Constantly, throughout the game, an umpire will be drawing from what he has retained from the baseball rule book when he is trying to make the right call. When information in the rule book is in language that is convoluted and blurred, the reader will retain convoluted and blurry information. Information that is randomly scattered through-out the rule book complicates the reader's ability to apply a complete ruling. With this dubious information, the umpire is then asked to correctly retain, recall and apply all of the pertinent rulings instantaneously on the field. Now you know why some umpires make confusing and arbitrary rulings during a baseball game.

Baseball Rules in Black and White realizes uncertain information produces questionable results, but excellent information produces exceptional results. *NFHS Baseball*

Rules in Black and White: 2019 – 2020 includes several new chapters. There is a new chapter on catches and two new chapters on dead balls that include awards and penalties.

NFHS Baseball Rules in Black and White: 2019 – 2020 covers the most frequently called and intricate rules of high school baseball. Chapters are listed in alphabetical order with related rulings to each chapter listed as sub-headings. This allows you to quickly target the exact ruling or related ruling's location and go there. Once you find your ruling or related ruling, you will then see directly below it whether it is an immediate or delayed dead ball, how many bases to award, do the runners return, exceptions, examples, and explanations. We have included many of the additional rulings that can or could apply to the original ruling. There are also author's notes and suggestions to help you gain a better understanding of the complex rules. In *NFHS Baseball Rules in Black and White: 2019 – 2020* rules are formatted logically in order of sequence and importance.

A high school umpire, coach, player, or fan who has come up through the ranks of Little League or one of the dozens of other youth leagues may be well versed in their own specific official rule set. These same individuals quickly realize that they are well behind the learning curve when it comes to understanding the many nuances of the official high school rule book. Because NFHS Baseball Rules in Black and White: 2019 – 2020 presents these nuances in an easy to find, read, understand, retain, and apply format, a steep learning curve quickly becomes a level playing field.

If you are an experienced high school umpire, coach, player, or parent, this book will be extremely helpful. If you are an umpire, coach, player, or parent new to the game of high school baseball, this book is mandatory reading. Without this book, you are in store for difficult years of learning as you umpire, coach, play, or watch the game of high school baseball. *NFHS Baseball Rules in Black and White: 2019 – 2020* has been written and formatted so that everyone can gain an improved understanding of the rules of high school baseball well before the season starts.

Specifically, for umpires, this book and its unique enhanced format is designed to strengthen your high school baseball rule knowledge and retention. These benefits stimulate game day recognition and application on the field, thereby reducing hesitation. Best of all, it improves your ability to articulate what the ruling actually says, when needed.

Baseball teams and umpires are always striving to get better. I believe the same standard should be applied to baseball rule books. Producing an improved educational resource with every edition of Baseball Rules in Black and White is our objective. No one associated with the game of baseball should settle for less.

Balk

Infractions by pitchers are common and it is important to know what constitutes a balk, but also what it is not a balk. A balk in baseball is one of the most subtle, obvious, and random infractions in the game today, so much so that at every level of the game of baseball, few if any can agree on whether a balk infraction did or did not happen. This illuminates the importance of clearly being able to understand the exact definitions of the rulings for a balk at each specific level of play in order to correctly call a balk during a game.

Definition of a Balk

- The pitcher holding the ball is in contact with the pitcher's plate and commits an illegal act with runner(s) on base.

Rule 2: Section 3: Page 16.
Rule 6: Section 1: Article 1, Page 39.

Results:

1. It is an immediate dead ball.

Rule 5: Section 1: Dead Ball Table, Activity 20, Page 37.
Rule 6: Section 1: Article 3, Penalty, Page 40.

2. Each runner is awarded one base.

Rule 2: Section 3: Page 16.
Rule 8: Section 3: Article 1-a, Page 51.

3. When there are no runners on base during an illegal act, a ball is awarded to the batter.

Rule 6: Section 1: Article 3, Penalty, Page 40.

Definition of an Illegal Pitch

- An illegal pitch is considered an illegal act by the pitcher. With no runners on base, a ball will be awarded to the batter.

Rule 2: Section 18: Page 20.
Rule 5: Section 1: Activity 1, Page 36.

Penalty: It's an immediate dead ball.

Rule 6: Section 1: Article 3, Penalty, Page 40.

It is a Balk When:

• The pitcher, after bringing his hands together, turns his shoulders, during or after his stretch.

> Rule 6: Section 1: Article 1, Page 39, 40.

• The pitcher feints toward the batter or throws to first base while in contact with the pitcher's plate.

> Rule 6: Section 2: Article 4-a, Page 42.

> Feint: any motion excluding the turning of the head by the pitcher that can be associated with pitch or a throw that is used to deceive a runner.

• The pitcher, in contact with the pitching rubber, drops the ball and the ball stops in fair territory.

> Rule 6: Section 2: Article 4-a, Page 42.

> Exception: When the dropped ball rolls foul it will be called a ball.

> Rule 6: Section 1: Article 4, Page 40.

• The pitcher throws or feints to either put out or drive back a runner without his non-pivot foot stepping directly towards the base.

> Rule 6: Section 2: Article 4-b, Page 42.

• The pitcher throws or feints to an unoccupied base.

> Rule 6: Section 2: Article 4-b, Page 42.

> Exception: It is not a balk when the pitcher is trying to put out or drive back a runner at or from an unoccupied base.

> Rule 6: Section 2: Article 4-b, Page 42.

• The pitcher, during his stretch, stops and starts his motion while going to his set position.

> Rule 6: Section 1: Article 3, Page 40.

- The pitcher, after coming set, begins his delivery then stops and starts (double set) his motion.

  Rule 6: Section 2: Article 4-d, Page 42.

- The pitcher, after his stretch, does not come to a complete and discernable STOP when his hands are brought together.

  Rule 6: Section 1: Article 3 Page 40.

- The pitcher, when disengaging the pitcher's plate, does not step backward off the pitcher's plate with his pivot foot first.

  Rule 6: Section 1: Article 3 Page 40.

- The pitcher comes to a stop after his stretch and his hands, ball, and glove are at or above his chin.

  Rule 6: Section 1: Article 3 Page 40.

- The pitcher fails to pitch after the entire non-pivot foot moves past the back edge of the pitcher's plate.

  Exception: It is not a balk when after the entire non-pivot foot moves past the back edge of the pitcher's plate, the pitcher makes a legal attempt to pick off or drive back a runner at second base only.

  Rule 6: Section 2: Article 4-f, Page 42.

Section Continued on Page 6

- The pitcher, while not holding the ball with runner(s) on base, does the following:

1. Feints a pitch.
2. Straddles or touches pitcher's plate.
3. Stands within approximately five feet of the pitcher's plate.

Rule 6: Section 2: Article 5, Page 42 – 43.

Authors Note: During a hidden ball trick, the defense may attempt to fool the runner and tag him while off the bag. When the pitcher is without the ball and standing within five feet of the pitcher's plate during the hidden ball trick, it is a balk. When the runner is tagged, he would not be out, it is a balk, and all runners would be awarded one base.

Rule 6: Section 2: Article 5, Page 42 – 43.

Illegal Acts

* With runners on base the pitcher makes an illegal act.

Rule 2: Section 3: Page 16.

Result: It's an immediate dead ball.

Rule 6: Section 1: Article 3-Penalty, Page 40.

Note: When an illegal act by the pitcher happens with runner(s) on base it is considered a balk.

Rule 2: Article 18: Page 20.
Rule 6: Section 2: Article 4-c, Page 42.

* With no runners on base the pitcher makes an illegal pitch, it is considered an illegal act by the pitcher and a ball will be awarded to the batter.

Rule 2: Section 18: Page 20.
Rule 5: Section 1: Activty-1, Page 36.

Result: It's an immediate dead ball.

Rule 6: Section 1: Article 3-Penalty, Page 40.

* Illegal acts include:

1. Defacing the ball by applying foreign substance.

Rule 6: Section 2: Article 1-a, Page 41.

2. Defacing the ball by spitting on ball or glove.

Rule 6: Section 2: Article 1-b, Page 41.

3. Defacing the ball by rubbing the ball.

Rule 6: Section 2: Article 1-c, Page 41.

4. Defacing the ball by rubbing dirt on ball.

Rule 6: Section 2: Article 1-a – d, Page 41.
Rule 6: Section 2: Article 1: Penalties a – d, Page 41.

Ruling Continued on Page 8

Penalties for 1 – 4:

a. Immediate Dead Ball.

b. Possible pitcher ejection.
> Rule 6: Section 2: Article 1-a – d, Penalty, Page 41.

Note: A defaced ball discovered after a pitch is an illegal pitch.
> Rule 6: Section 2: Article 1-a – d, Penalty, Page 41.

5. Taking pitching hand directly from mouth to ball, without wiping off hand before touching ball.
> Rule 6: Section 2: Article 1-e, Page 41.

Penalty: Each time the pitcher fails to wipe off before touching ball, a ball is awarded to batter.
> Rule 6: Section 2: Article 1-e, Penalty, Page 41.

6. Pitcher wearing items distracting to the batter on hand, wrist, or arms.
> Rule 6: Section 2: Article 1-f, Page 41.

Penalty: The umpire will have sole authority of judging when the item is distracting or is to be removed.
> Rule 6: Section 2: Article 1-f, Penalty, Page 41.

7. Pitcher is wearing or places tape, bandages, or foreign material on his throwing hand that can come in contact with the ball.
> Rule 6: Section 2: Article 1-g, Page 41.

8. Pitcher has white or gray on his glove.
> Rule 6: Section 2: Article 1-h, Page 41.

9. Pitcher has white or gray exposed sleeves.
> Rule 6: Section 2: Article 1-i, Page 41.

For 5 - 9, illegal acts will be corrected before next pitch.
> Rule 6: Section 2: Article 1, Penalty, Page 41.

It is Not a Balk When:

* The pitcher from the set position legally steps and throws "with no play at an occupied base" to either the second baseman, third baseman, or shortstop, who are playing away from the occupied base.

    Result: The pitcher while in contact with the pitcher's plate can pitch to, throw to, step toward, or feint to "an occupied" second or third base.

    Rule 6: Section 2: Article 4-e, Page 42.

    Explanation: Throwing to a fielder away from an occupied base is the equivalent to feinting to the base.

* The pitcher stops or hesitates his delivery because:

    1. The batter steps out of the batter's box with both feet.
        Result: A strike will be called on the batter.

    2. The batter steps out of the batter's box with one foot.
        Result: No penalty on either the batter or pitcher.

    3. The batter raises his hand to request time.
        Result: No penalty on either the batter or pitcher.

    Rule 6: Section 2: Article 4-d-1, Page 42.

* The offense purposely causes a pitcher to balk by:
    1. Calling time.
    2. Any voice commands.
    3. Any action.

    Rule 3: Section 3: Article 1-n, Page 30.

    Result: It is a delayed dead ball.

    Rule 5: Section 1: Article 2-d, Page 38.

Section Continued on Page 10

- A pitcher first moves his pivot foot backwards to legally disengage from the pitcher's plate. The pitcher can then legally:
  1. Throw or feint to a base.
  2. Field a batted or thrown ball.

  Rule 6: Section 1: Article 3, Page 40.

- A pitcher makes a legal jump step, as long as the lead foot gains some distance in the direction towards the base to which the throw is made.

  Rule 6: Section 1: Article 3, Page 40.

- The pitcher, while in contact with the pitcher's plate and prior to beginning his delivery motion, does the following:
  1. Turns on his pivot foot.
  2. Lift his pivot foot in a jump turn, while gaining distance with the non-pivot foot when either throwing or feinting.

     Result: He can legally disengage.

  Rule 6: Section 1: Article 3, Page 40.

- The pitcher turns his shoulders prior to beginning his stretch, while in contact with the pitching rubber.

  Rule 6: Section 1: Article 1, Page 39.

Author's Summary, Balk

• Pitching regulations begin when the pitcher contacts the pitcher's plate.

Rule 6: Section 1: Article 1, Page 39.

• In high school, a balk is an immediate dead ball.

Rule 5: Section 1: Activity 20, Page 37.

Result: Call time; it is a no pitch. Should a pitch that was called a balk be hit into play, the play is nullified, and all runners are awarded one base.

Rule 5: Section 1: Article 1-k, Award 20, Page 37.

• When the pitcher has legally disengaged the pitcher's plate, he is considered a fielder. All restrictions as a pitcher no longer apply.

Rule 6: Section 1: Article 5, Page 41.

Exception: When a runner or umpire is hit by a batted ball and for the sole purpose of judging the interference ruling, the pitcher has legally disengaged the pitcher's plate, he is not considered a fielder when the batted ball passes him.

Rule 8: Section 4: Article 2-k, Page 55.

• The pitcher, in the set position, after separating his hands from the ball, can legally do one of these three things:

1. Pitch.

Rule 6: Section 2: Article 4-e, Page 42.

2. Make a legal attempt to pick off or drive back a runner or step towards and feint a throw to occupied second or third base.

Rule 6: Section 2: Article 4-e, Page 42.

3. Legally disengage pitcher's plate.

Rule 6: Section 2: Article 3, Page 40.

Author's Notes, Balk

In high school baseball, particularly at the lower divisions and levels of play, balks frequently are not called. There are both very good reasons for this and very bad outcomes from it. The ability of the players to execute the components of the game of baseball dictates the frequency of when an umpire will call a balk. Here are a few very good reasons that support this:

1. A game might be in the second inning, an hour-fifteen has already passed, and the score is 24 – 0.
2. Pitchers do not have the skill set to execute legal pitches consistently.
3. Both coaching staffs, fans, and umpires recognize what the pitchers are not capable of doing.
4. The players recognize what they are not capable of doing.

Calling balks in these types of games adds misery on top of bad play. On the other side of the argument here are the bad outcomes:

1. Not calling an infraction goes against everything umpires are taught. Umpires should not selectively choose which rules to call or not call.
2. By not calling a balk, eventually you are going to be called out by someone.
3. In the next game, when the next umpiring crew does call it a balk, you will have set a precedent they are unaware of. They are surely going to hear that the last umpires didn't call it.
4. Allowing a pitcher to get away with a balk, you are doing him and his team a disfavor. Eventually it will get called, hopefully it's not when they are in the playoffs.

- One of the most frequently overlooked balks in high school baseball at all levels:
  1. The pitchers glove is at or above his chin when coming set.

Rule 6: Section 1: Article 3, Page 40.

Bottom line, it is the umpire's experience and discretion that ultimately makes the call.

Base Running Awards and Appeals

When an infraction or a batted or thrown ball goes out of play, what are the appropriate base award to give to the base runners? Rulings are listed under one base, two base, and three base awards in order to connect similar infractions with similar awards. Base running appeals have specific protocol in order for the appeal to be legal, and when the specific protocol is not followed, the appeal is not upheld. Appeals can also impact whether or not a run is scored after a third out is made. These are just few of the many reasons for understanding exactly what an appeal ruling is stating.

One Base Award When:

- A balk happens.

  Rule 8: Section 3: Article 1-a, Page 51.

  Result: It is an immediate dead ball.

  Rule 5: Section 1, Dead Ball Table, Activity 20, Page 37.
  Rule 6: Section 1: Article 3, Penalty, Page 40.

  Note: Runner's base awards are from bases occupied at the time of the infraction.

  Rule 8: Section 2: One Base Award Table, 1 (runners), Page 50.

- A batter or his clothing is hit by a pitch, and he is not swinging to hit the ball.

  Rule 8: Section 1: Article 1-d, Page 46.

  Result: It is an immediate dead ball.

  Rule 5: Section 1: Dead Ball Table, Activity 2, Page 36.

  Note: Base awards are from the time of pitch.

  Rule 8: Section 2: One Base Awards Table, Base (batter) 4, Page 50.

  Exception: A batter is not awarded first base when he allows the ball to hit him. It is an immediate dead ball and would be either a ball or a strike.

  Rule 8: Section 1: Article 1-d-1, Page 46.
  Rule 5: Section 1: Dead Ball Table, Activity 2, Page 36.

- A runner is forced by:
  1. A batter receiving a walk.
  2. A batter or his clothing is hit by a pitch.
  3. A fair-batted ball becomes dead.

  Rule 8: Section 3: Article 1-b, Page 51.

  Examples for 3:
  1. Balk.

  Rule 5: Section 1: Dead Ball Table, Activity 20, Page 37.

Ruling Continued on Page 17

2. Umpire hit by a batted ball before it touches a fielder or passes any fielder other than the pitcher.

> Rule 5: Section 1: Dead Ball Table, Activity 14, Page 36.

• A pitcher while in contact with the pitcher's plate, pitches or throws a ball that:

1. Goes into stand or benches.

2. Goes over, through or lodges in a fence or backstop.

3. Touches a spectator.

4. Lodges in catcher's or umpire's equipment.

> Rule 8: Section 3: Article 3-d, Page 51.

Results:

1. All four actions are immediate dead balls.

> Rule 5: Section 1: Dead Ball Table, Activity & Award 16, Page 36.

2. When a pitch goes out of play, base awards are from the time of the pitch.

> Rule 8: Section 2: One Base Awards Table, 2 (runners), Page 50.

3. When a throw goes out of play, base awards are from the time of the throw.

> Rule 8: Section 2: One Base Awards Table, 3 (runners), Page 50.

• With less than two outs, a fair fly ball, foul fly ball, or line drive is caught while the defensive player unintentionally continues with both feet, or falls into dead ball territory.

> Rule 8: Section 3: Article 3-d, Page 51 – 52.

Result: It is an immediate dead ball. Runners are awarded one base from bases occupied at the time of the pitch.

> Rule 5: Section 1: Dead Ball Table, Activity 18, Page 36.
> Rule 8: Section 2: One Base Award Table, 4 (runners), Page 50.
> Rule 5: Section 1: Dead Ball Table, Award 18, Page 36.

Section Continued on Page 18

- The batter is obstructed and a runner that is attempting to steal or that is forced by another runner has not advanced at the end of the playing action.

Rule 8: Section 3: Article 1-c, Page 51.
Rule 5: Section 1: Dead Ball Table, Award 3, Page 37.

Result: It is a delayed dead ball, let the play finish.

Rule 5: Section 1: Dead Ball Table, Activity 3, Page 37.

Note: Three possible ways a catcher can obstruct a runner:

1. Catcher steps on or across home plate.

2. Catcher pushes the batter to reach a pitch.

3. Catcher pushes the bat.

Rule 8: Section 3: Article 1-c, Page 51.

Two Base Award When:

• A ball goes out of play as a result of the first play (release of the ball) by an infielder.

Rule 8: Section 3: Article 5, Page 52.

Result: Immediate dead ball. Award two bases all runners, including the batter, from their locations at the time of the pitch.

Rule 5: Section 1: Dead Ball Table, Activity 15, Page 36.
Rule 8: Section 3: Article 5, Page 52.
Rule 8: Section 2: Two Base Award Table, 5 (batter & runner), Page 50.

Note: The act of fielding is not considered a play.

Rule 8: Section 3: Article 5-b, Page 52.

• A ball goes out of play after every runner including the batter runner has advanced one base (prior to the first throw by an infielder).

Rule 8: Section 3: Article 5, Page 52.

Result: Immediate dead ball. Two base award from their locations at the (time of the throw).

Rule 5: Section 1: Activity 15, Page 36.
Rule 8: Section 3: Article 5-b, Page 52.
Rule 8: Section 2: Two Base Award Table, (batter & runner), Page 50.

• A throw by an outfielder or secondary play by an infielder that goes out of play.

Rule 8: Section 3: Article 5, Page 52.

Result: Immediate dead ball. Award two bases from runner's locations at the time of the throw.

Rule 5: Section 1: Activity 15, Page 36.
Rule 8: Section 2: Two Base Award Table, 6 (batter & runner), Page 50

Section Continued on Page 20

- A live thrown ball or pitch is touched by:
  1. An illegal glove or catcher's mitt.

     Rule 8: Section 3: Article 3-c-1, Page 51.

     Results:

     a. Delayed dead ball.

     Rule 8: Section 3: Article 4, Page 52.
     Rule 5: Section 1: Delayed Dead Ball Table, Activity 6, Page 37.

     b. Award two bases from runner's locations occupied at the (time of the infraction).

     Rule 8: Section 2: Two Base Award Table, 3 (batter & runner), Page 50.

     c. Runners advancing to or beyond base award, the infraction is ignored.

     Rule 8: Section 3: Article 4. Page 52.

     d. Runners advance beyond their base award at their own risk.

     Rule 8: Section 3: Article 4. Page 52.

  2. A player's detached equipment that is held, thrown, tossed or kicked.

     Rule 8: Section 3: Article 3-c-1, Page 51.

     Results:

     a. Delayed dead ball.

     Rule 8: Section 3: Article 4, Page 52.
     Rule 5: Section 1: Delayed Dead Ball Table, Activity 6, Page 37.

     b. Award two bases from runner's locations at the (time of the infraction).

     Rule 8: Section 2: Two Base Award Table, 4-(batter & runner), Page 50.

     c. Runners advancing to or beyond base award, the infraction is ignored.

     Rule 8: Section 3: Article 4. Page 52.

     d. Runners advance beyond their base award at their own risk.

     Rule 8: Section 3: Article 4. Page 52.

- A fair batted or thrown ball becomes dead by:

  1. Bouncing over, through or lodges in a fence.
     Rule 8: Section 3: Article 3-c-2, Page 51.
     Rule 5: Section 1: Dead Ball Table, Activity 12, Page 36.

  2. Going into stands, dugout or player's bench.
     Rule 8: Section 3: Article 3-c-2, Page 51.
     Rule 5: Section 1: Dead Ball Table, Activity 12, Page 36.

  3. Lodges in a defensive player's or umpires equipment or uniform.
     Rule 8: Section 3: Article 3-c, Page 51.

     Results:

     a. All three are an immediate dead ball.

     b. All three are two base awards from time of the pitch.
        Rule 5: Section 1: Activity 12, Page 36.
        Rule 5: Section 1: Dead Ball Table, Activity 12, Page 36.
        Rule 8: Section 2: Two Base Award Table, 1 (batter & runner), Page 50.

     Exception: When the ball is thrown by the pitcher in contact with pitcher's plate, it is a one base award.
     Rule 8: Section 3: Article 3-d, Page 51.

- A throw goes into dead ball territory, and two runners are between bases, the lead runner is awarded two bases and the trail runner one base.

Rule 8: Section 3: Article 3-c-3, Page 51

Section Continued on Page 22

- A batted ball is caught and a runner is prevented from returning to a missed base or one left too early because a live thrown ball goes into dead ball territory.

Rule 8: Section 3: Article 5, Page 52.

Result:

a.   It is an immediate dead ball.

b.   Two bases awarded from runner's locations at the time of the pitch.

Rule 5: Section 1: Dead Ball Table, Activity 12, Page 36.
Rule 8: Section 3: Article 5, Page 52.

Three Base Award When:

* A defensive player touches a batted fair ball with an illegal glove or catcher's mitt, and the ball is:
  1. On or over fair ground.
  2. Fair, while on or over foul ground.
  3. Over foul ground which could become fair.

  Rule 8: Section 3: Article 3-b, Page 51.

  Results:
  a. It is a delayed dead ball.

  Rule 8: Section 3: Article 4, Page 52.
  Rule 5: Section 1: Delayed Dead Ball Table, Activity 5, Page 37.

  b. Three bases awarded from (runner's locations at the time of the infraction).

  Rule 8: Section 2: Three Base Award, (batter & runner), Page 50.

  c. When runners advance to or beyond base award, the infraction is ignored.

  Rule 8: Section 3: Article 4. Page 52.

  d. Runners advance beyond their base award at their own risk.

  Rule 8: Section 3: Article 4. Page 52.

* A defensive player touches a (fair-batted ball) with detached equipment which is held, thrown, tossed or kicked, and the ball is:
  1. On or over fair ground.
  2. Fair, on or over foul ground.
  3. Over foul ground which could become fair.

  Rule 8: Section 3: Article 3-b, Page 51.

  Results:
  a. It is a delayed dead ball.

  Rule 8: Section 3: Article 4, Page 52.
  Rule 5: Section: Delayed Dead Ball Table-Activity 5, Page 37

Ruling Continued on Page 24

b. Three bases awarded from runner's (locations at the time of the infraction).

Rule 8: Section 2: Three Base Award-(batter & runner), Page 50.

c. When runners advance to or beyond base award, the infraction is ignored.

Rule 8: Section 3: Article 4. Page 52.

d. Runners advance beyond their base award at their own risk.

Rule 8: Section 3: Article 4. Page 52.

Time of Base Award

- Bases will be awarded from the time of the pitch when a pitched or batted ball becomes a dead ball before either of the following actions:

  1. The defense makes a throw.

  2. The pitcher is in contact with the pitcher's plate ready for the next pitch.

  Rule 8: Section 3: Article 5-b, Page 52.

- Base award is from the time of the throw for the following infractions:

  1. Throw from the pitcher's plate goes out of play.

  Rule 8: Section 3: Article 3-d, Page 51.

  2. Any secondary play or throw that goes out of play.

  Rule 8: Section 3: Article 5, Page 52.

  3. Any throw by an outfielder that goes out of play.

  Rule 8: Section 3: Article 5, Page 52.

- Base award is from the time of the infraction for the following infractions:

  1. Balk.

  Rule 8: Section 3: Article 5-a, Page 52.

  2. Live thrown or pitched ball touched by illegal glove or mitt.

  Rule 8: Section 3: Article 5-a, Page 52.

  3. Live thrown or pitched ball touched by thrown, tossed, kicked or held detached equipment.

  Rule 8: Section 3: Article 5-a, Page 52.

  4. Fair batted ball contacted with detached player equipment or illegal glove/mitt.

  Rule 8: Section 3: Article 5-a, Page 51.

Appeal Procedures for Base Running

• Defense must appeal before the next legal or illegal pitch.

• Defense must appeal before the end of the inning and before all defensive players have left fair territory.

• Defense must appeal before an intentional base on balls.

• Defense must appeal before the next play or attempted play.

Rule 8: Section 2: Articles-1 – 5-Penalty, Page 47, 48.

Exception: When the offense initiates a play before the next pitch the defense can still appeal.

Rule 8: Section 2: Article 5-Penalty, Page 47 & 48.

Live Ball Appeal

- During a live ball any fielder possessing the ball can appeal by:
  1. Touching a missed base.
  2. Touching a base left early on a caught fly ball.
  3. Tagging the runner who committed the violation.

Rule 8: Section 2: Article 6-b, Page 48.
Rule 8: Section 2: Article 5-Penalty, Page 47 & 48.

Dead Ball Appeal

- Once all runners reach their base and time has been called, a coach or defensive player with or without the ball can verbally appeal a missed base or a base left early on a caught fly ball. The umpire can then make a ruling.

Rule 8: Section 2: Article 6-c, Page 48.

- When the ball becomes dead while the runner is on or past the next base, he cannot return to retouch the base left early or missed and can therefore be called out on a legal appeal.

Rule 8: Section 2: Article 5, Page 47.

Missed Base & Failure to Tag Up Appeals

• When a runner misses touching a base, the defense can appeal.

Rule 8: Section 2: Article 6-a-1, Page 48.

• When a defensive player is attempting to catch a fly ball, before the ball is first touched, and a runner leaves the base early while tagging up, the defense can appeal.

Rule 8: Section 2: Article 6-a-2, Page 48.

• A live ball appeal is when any fielder, during a live ball, while holding the ball, touches the base or tags the runner that is being appealed.

Notes:
1. Runners may advance during a live ball appeal.
2. Time out can be requested and granted during a live ball appeal.

Rule 8: Section 2: Article 6-e, Page 48.

• A dead ball appeal can be made:
1. When the ball has gone out of play, runners must first attain their appropriate bases before an appeal can be made.

Rule 8: Section 2: Article 6-c, Page 48.

2. After time is called.

Rule 8: Section 2: Article 6-c, Page 48.

• Any coach or defensive player, with or without the ball, can make a verbal appeal regarding a runner missing a base or leaving early on a caught fly ball.

Rule 8: Section 2: Article 6-c, Page 48.

Section Continued on Page 30

- With two outs, when appealing a missed base or leaving a base early, any runs scored by trailing runners would not count.

  Rule 8: Section 2: Article 6-k, Page 49.

- With two outs, when the appeal was the base that the batter-runner or runner was forced to advance and missed, no runs would score.

  Rule 8: Section 2: Article 6-k, Page 49.

  Example: With bases loaded and two outs, the batter hits a triple, but the forced runner who was at first base missed second base and on a legal appeal is called out. No runs would score.

  Rule 8: Section 2: Article 6-k, Page 49.

- When a runner leaves early on a caught fly ball, then returns to retag it is a time play.

  Rule 8: Section 2: Article 6-h, Page 48.

1. All runners who score in front of the appealed runner and prior to the legal third-out appeal would count.

  Rule 8: Section 2: Article 6-h, Page 48.

- Multiple appeals may be granted.

  Rule 8: Section 2: Article 6-f, Page 48.

- An appeal must be granted, even when the missed base happened before or after an award.

  Rule 8: Section 2: Article 6-g, Page 48.

- Any appeal on the last play of the game must be made while the umpires are still on the field.

  Rule 8: Section 2: Article 6-j, Page 49.

Third Out Tag-Up Appeals

• When an appeal for a runner leaving a base early is the third out, all runs scored by runners ahead of the appealed runner and scored before the legal appeal would count.

   Examples:

   1. With one out and runners at second and third, the batter hits a fly ball to center field that is caught for the second out. The runner at third base tags up and scores, but the runner from second base leaves early and goes to third base. The defense legally appeals.

      Result: The appeal is the third out, therefore, the run that scored from third ahead of the appeal counts.

   2. With one-out, runners at first and third, batter hits a fly ball to left field that is caught for the second out. Both runners tag up but the runner from first base leaves early and is thrown out before the runner from third base can score.

      Result: Leaving a base early is a time play. Since the run did not score before a legal appeal, it does not count.

      Rule 8: Section 2: Article 6-h, Page 48 & 49.

• With two-outs, when the base missed was the first base the batter or runner were forced to advance, no runs are counted.

   Rule 8: Section 2: Article 6-k, Page 49.

Ruling Continued on Page 32

Examples:

1. With one out and bases loaded, the batter hits a deep fly ball to left-center field that is caught for the second out. All runners tag up, and the runner from third base scores. The runner from second base, while rounding third base, misses the bag but scores. The defense legally appeals the missed base.

   Result: The runner from second base is called out for missing third base. Since he was forced to run, no runs score.

2. With two outs and a runner at first, the batter get a hit deep down the right fieldline that bounces away from the fielder. The runner from first base scores, but the batter-runner misses first base on his way to second. The missed base is legally appealed.

   Result: Since the batter is forced to run and the appeal is the third out, no runs score.

Rule 9: Section 1: Exception-d, Page 56.
Rule 8: Section 2: Article 6-k, Page 49.

- During any baserunning appeal, runs scored by the following runner(s) would not count.

  Example: With two-out and runners at second and third the batter hits an inside the park home run, but the runner at second base missed third base.

  Result: On appeal the runner from second base is out for missing third and the batter-runner score does not count.

Rule 8: Section 2: Article 6-k, Page 49.

Author's Summary:

- With a missed-base third-out appeal, when the base missed was the first base which the batter or runner was forced to advance, no runs would score.

- With a third-out appeal for a runner leaving early on a tag-up, all runs that score ahead of the appealed runner and scored ahead of the legal appeal would count.

- When the appeal is the third out, runners scoring behind the base-running infraction do not count.

Runner Returning to Touch Missed Base or Tag Up

- A runner returning to touch a missed base or a base left early while tagging up, will retouch bases in reverse order.

  Rule 8: Section 2: Article 2, Page 47.

- Any runner who has missed a base may not retouch it when a trailing runner has scored.

  Rule 8: Section 2: Article 3, Page 47.

- Runners returning to touch a missed base or a base they left early while tagging up must do so immediately.

  Rule 8: Section 2: Article 5, Page 47.

- Runners returning to tag a base can be put out by being tagged or by a defender touching the base before the runner does.

  Rule 8: Section 2: Article 6-k, Page 49.

A Player Cannot Return to a Missed Base or to Tag Up When:

- A runner may not return to tag for a missed base or for leaving early on a fly ball when:
  1. The ball becomes dead.
  2. The runner has left the field of play.
  3. A trailing runner has scored.

Rule 8: Section 2: Article 6-d-2, Page 48.

Batting Out of Order

For years as an umpire, I found the rule language in official rule books about batting out of order impossible to understand. We have changed that and provided content regarding batting out of order that is reader friendly and easily retained. We have also created examples of batting out of order scenarios that can and do happen to define and illustrate the infraction and the correct ruling that would apply. We have been able to create content that is no longer complicated or confusing, but rather straightforward and undemanding. No matter how screwed up the batting order gets, you will now know what to do.

Legal Appeal for Batting Out of Order

• For a batting-out-of-order appeal to be legal, after the illegal batter has completed his at-bat (whether he gets on base or not) the appeal has to be made before one of these four things happen:

1. The first legal or illegal pitch is made to the next batter.

2. A play or attempted play is made.

3. An intentional walk.

4. Infielders leaving the diamond when a half inning is ending.

Rule 7: Section 1: Article 2-Penalty-2: Page 43.

Rulings for Batting Out of Order

•   While an improper batter is at-bat, all outs stand and runner advances are legal.

Rule 7: Section 1: Article 1: Page 43.

•   When an improper batter is discovered by either team before completing his at-bat, the proper batter will replace the improper batter and assume the improper batter's strike count.

Rule 7: Section 1: Article 1: Page 43.

•   After an improper batter completes his at-bat, his time at-bat is legal and he will become a proper batter when:

1. He becomes a runner, and a legal or illegal pitch is delivered to the next batter.
2. He is put out, and a legal or illegal pitch is delivered to the next batter.
3. His at-bat is followed by an intentional base on balls.
4. All fielders leave the diamond at the end of the half inning before an appeal is made.

> Note: After an improper batter completes his at-bat and any one of the four above actions take place, the improper batter becomes the new legalized proper batter, therefore making his time at-bat legal.

Rule 7: Section 1: Article 2-Penalty-3: Page 43, 44.

Section Continued on Page 40

- When an improper batter completes his at-bat and there is either no appeal or an illegal appeal, the improper batter becomes the new legalized proper batter.

  Rule 7: Section 1: Article 2-Penalty-5: Page 44.

  Note: The batting order will then continue with the next batter that follows the new legalized proper batter. For a batter to be legal, he must follow the last legal batter.

  Rule 7: Section 1: Article 2-Penalty-5: Page 44.
  Rule 7: Section 1: Article 1: Page 43.

- When an improper batter completes his at-bat and is discovered on a legal appeal, the proper batter who should have batted is called out for not batting in turn.

  Rule 7: Section 1: Article 2-Penalty-1: Page 43.

  Result: All runners return to bases occupied at the time of the pitch.

  Rule 7: Section 1: Article 2-Penalty-2: Page 43.

- When a proper batter is called out for not batting in turn, the next batter will be whoever would have followed that proper batter in the batting order.

  Rule 7: Section 1: Article 2-Penalty-4: Page 44.

- When a batter's turn at-bat happens while he is a base runner due to batting out of order, he is to remain a baserunner and is not called out for not batting.

  Rule 7: Section 1: Article 2-Note: Page 44.

Author's Examples, Batting Out of Order

• The official lineup card reads the three-spot batter should be batting, but the four-spot batter is at-bat instead and has a pitch count of one ball, two strikes. Before the four-spot batter completes his at-bat, the offense or defense can and does inform (appeals) the umpire.

> Result: The illegal four-spot batter does not complete his at-bat, the proper three-spot batter who should have been batting replaces the illegal four-spot batter and assumes the improper batter's pitch count.
>
> Rule 7: Section 1: Article 1: Page 43.

• The four-spot batter gets a base hit, but it is discovered on a legal appeal that he batted out of order. The three-spot batter should have batted.

> Result: The proper three-spot batter is called out for failing to bat in his correct spot. The four-spot batter that just illegally batted would then return to bat in his legal batting spot, following the three-spot batter. All runners return to bases occupied at the time of the pitch.
>
> Rule 7: Section 1: Article 2-Penalty-2: Page 43.

• The four-spot batter bats out of order and gets a base hit. The three-spot batter then comes to bat, a pitch is thrown, and then an appeal is made.

Ruling Continued on Page 42

Result: The appeal is denied because a pitch was thrown. The four-spot batter becomes the new legalized proper batter runner. Because the four-spot batter is now the last legal proper to bat, the five-spot batter would replace the three-spot batter at-bat and assume the three-spot's pitch count.

Rule 7: Section 1: Article 2-Penalty-5: Page 44.
Rule 7: Section 1: Article 1: Page 43.

- The four-spot batter bats out of order ahead of the three-spot batter and gets thrown out at first base. The three-spot batter comes to the plate and a pitch is thrown.

  Result: Even though the four-spot was thrown out, there was no appeal and a pitch was thrown, which now makes the four-spot batter the last legal proper batter and his time at-bat becomes official. The five-spot batter would then take the three-spot batter place at-bat and assume his pitch count.

  Rule 7: Section 1: Article 2-Penalty-3: Page 43 & 44.

- When a batter bats ahead of several batters in the lineup, for example: the eight-spot batter is batting in the three-spot batter's position in the batting order, various things can happen. The scenarios and results listed below:

  1. The eight-spot batter is discovered while still at-bat.

     Result: The proper three-spot batter would replace the eight-spot at-bat and assume the eight-spot's pitch count.

     Rule 7: Section 1: Article 1: Page 43.

Ruling Continued on Page 43

2. After the eight-spot batter reaches base, a legal appeal is made.

> Result: The three-spot batter is called out for failing to bat in his correct spot and the four-spot batter would become the next proper batter to bat.
>
> Rule 7: Section 1: Article 2- Penalty-4: Page 44.

3. After the eight-spot batter reaches base, either an illegal appeal or no appeal takes place.

> Result: The eight-spot batter then becomes a new legalized proper batter. When discovered, the nine-spot batter would become the next proper batter to bat.

Note: Batters in the four through seven spots lose their opportunity to bat. Should a newly legalized proper batter be on base when his turn at-bat happens, he will remain on-base with no penalty and whoever is listed as following him would bat.

> Rule 7: Section 2: Article 5-Note: Page 44.

Author's Summary, Batting Out of Order

• When an improper batter completes his at-bat and there is either no appeal or an illegal appeal, that improper batter then becomes the new legalized proper batter.

> Rule 7: Section 1: Article 2-Penalty-5, Page 44.

• The next proper batter will always be whoever follows the last proper or new legalized proper batter on the line-up card.

> Rule 7: Section 1: Article 1, Page 43.
> Rule 7: Section 1: Article 2-Penalty-4, Page 44.
> Rule 7: Section 1: Article 2-Penalty-5, Page 44.

• When an improper batter completes his at-bat and is either called out or becomes a runner, and the defense does one of the following:

1. Fails to appeal or makes an illegal appeal.

2. Throws a legal or illegal pitch.

3. An intentional walk or before the defense leaves the field.

> Result: Then the improper batter would then become the new legalized proper batter.
>
> Rule 7: Section 1: Article 2-Penalty-3. Page 43, 44.

Author's Note:

• An improper batter, when discovered while still batting, is not subject to penalty.

• Once the improper batter reaches first base, he is then subject to being called out on a legal appeal.

Catch

A simple as it may seem, the definition of a catch in baseball, and how it is written in official baseball rule books, turns what should be a simple matter into confusion and uncertainty. When a fielder gets a fly ball in his glove and travels several more steps and the ball falls to the ground, making a definitive ruling that is cloudy in your own mind is a recipe for disaster. We convert confusion and uncertainty into definitive clear basic English. So, when you make a ruling on the field, it is acquired from easily retained information that can be easily articulated to questioning players and coaches.

Definition of a Catch

• A catch is the act of a fielder securing possession of a live ball in flight in his hand or glove while firmly holding it.

> Exception: It is not a catch when the player uses his cap, protector, mask, pocket, or other parts of his uniform to trap the ball.
>> Rule 2: Section 9: Page 17 & 18.

• It is still considered a catch when, after the ball is in the defensive players' glove, he stops and begins to remove the ball from his glove then drops the ball.
>> Rule 2: Section 9: Page 17 & 18.

> The definition of a catch is the same when the defense is attempting a double play.
>> Rule 2: Section 9: Page 17 & 18.

> Author's Note: Voluntary release is the initial act of the defensive player removing the ball from his glove. Voluntary release also establishes a catch.

• It is a catch when the fielder catches a fair or foul ball then steps or falls into a dead ball area.

> Note: Running against is not considered falling into a dead ball boundary.
>> Rule 2: Section 9: Page 17 & 18.

• A foul tip is a legal catch when it goes directly into the catcher's hands (glove).
>> Rule 2: Section 16: Article 2: Page 19.

> Exception: It is not a catch if the player uses his cap, protector, mask, pocket, or other parts of his uniform to trap the ball.
>> Rule 2: Section 9: Page 17 & 18.

Definition of when a Fly Ball is not a Catch

- It is not a catch of a fly ball until the defensive player's continuing action is completed.

    Examples:

    1. A fly ball is not a catch when the ball is in the fielder's glove and while at full speed continues several more steps and then drops the ball from his glove.

    2. A fly ball is not a catch when the ball is in the fielder's glove and he runs into a wall or player and drops the ball.

    Rule 2: Section 9: Page 17 & 18.

- It is not a catch when a fielder touches a batted fly ball which then contacts an offensive player or umpire and is then caught by the defense.

    Rule 2: Section 9: Page 17 & 18.

Fielder Intentionally Drops a Fly Ball

- When any infielder intentionally drops a fair fly, line drive, or bunt in flight with at least one runner on and less than two outs, then:

  1. The ball is immediately dead.

  2. The batter-runner is out.

  3. Runner(s) will return to their bases.

Rule 5: Section 1: Dead ball Table-Activity 19, Page 36.

Rule 8: Section 4: Article 1-c, Page 53.

Fielder Allows Fly Ball to Drop Untouched

- When the infielder allows a fair fly, line drive, or bunt in flight to drop untouched to the ground, the batter is not out.

  Exception: When the Infield fly rule is in effect, batter-runner is out.

  Rule 8: Section 4: Article 1-c-1, Page 53.

Charged Conferences

How many charged conferences before the pitcher gets pulled in regulation play? How many charged conferences before a pitcher gets pulled in extra innings? If I don't use my charged conferences in regulation play, can I use them in extra innings? When do conference end? Easy enough simple questions with the answers collected, converted into basic English, and organized into an easy-to-find format.

Defense Conference Regulation Seven-Inning Game

- The defense gets three charged conferences to talk with any defensive players, not just the pitcher, without penalty.

Rule 3: Section 4: Article 1, Page 31.

1. Beginning with a fourth charged conference and every additional charged conference, the pitcher will be removed as pitcher for the remainder of the game.

Rule 3: Section 4: Article 1- Penalty, Page 31.

- A pitching change during the first three charged conferences or an injury time out are not considered a charged conference.

Rule 3: Section 4: Article 1, Page 31.

- Unused charged conferences in either regulation game or extra innings do not carry over.

Rule 3: Section 4: Article 1, Page 31.

Defensive Conference for Extra Innings

* The defense is allowed one charged conference without penalty in each extra inning.

Rule 3: Section 4: Article 1, Page 31.

1. With the second charged conference and every additional charged conference in each extra inning, the pitcher will be removed as pitcher for the remainder of the game.

Rule 3: Section 4: Article 1- Penalty, Page 31.

Defensive Conference Ends When:

- The charged conference is held in fair territory, as soon as the coach crosses the foul line.

Rule 3: Section 4: Article 3, Page 31.

- The charged conference is held in foul territory, as soon as the coach initially starts to return to the dugout.

Rule 3: Section 4: Article 3, Page 31.

Offensive Conference

- The offense is allowed one charged conference in each regulation inning and each extra inning.

   Rule 3: Section 4: Article 2, Page 31.

  1. All additional requests for a charged conference are to be denied.

   Rule 3: Section 4: Article 2, Page 31.

<u>Offensive Conference Ends When:</u>

- The coach initially starts his return to the dugout or coach's box.

Rule 3: Section 4: Article 4, Page 31.

- Coaches who have been confined to the bench, as soon as his team initially starts return to field.

Rule 3: Section 4: Article 4, Page 31.

Conference without Penalty

- During a team's charged conference, the other team may confer without being charged a conference.

  Rule 3: Section 4: Article 5, Page 31.

1. A team can confer during another team's charged conference without penalty as long as their conference concludes before or at the same time as the team holding a charged conference.

   Rule 3: Section 4: Article 5, Page 31.

Dead Ball Guide—Delayed

After decades of having this chapter's content offered only from the official rule book with seventy-six activities, awards, and penalties on two small pages. We have categorized the Delayed dead ball into specific categories so that you can quickly find what you are looking for. Is it a batted ball, a thrown ball, or is there interference or obstruction involved? These are the type of categories we have placed these ruling under so that makes your job of finding what you are looking for easier.

A Batted Ball is a Delayed Dead Ball When:

- A defensive player intentionally touches a batted ball with detached player equipment over fair ground or over foul ground which might become fair ball.

Rule 5: Section 1: DBT-Act. 5, Page 37.

> Result: Award batter-runner and runner(s) three bases when not made.

Rule 5: Section 1: DBT-Award 5, Page 37.

- A defensive player uses his illegal glove/mitt to hit a live ball.

Rule 5: Section 1: DBT-Act. 10, Page 37.

> Penalties:
> 1. Four bases for over-fence home run.
> 2. Three bases for other fair batted ball.
> 3. Two bases for thrown or pitched ball.

Rule 5: Section 1: DBT-Award 10, Page 37.

Interference is a Delayed Dead Ball When:

• The batter interferes with the catcher during an attempt to put out a runner at a base other than at home.

Rule 5: Section 1: DBT-Act. 1, Page 37.

Results:

1. When the attempt on the runner is unsuccessful, ball becomes dead. Batter is out and runners return.

Rule 5: Section 1: DBT-Penalty 1, Page 37.

2. When the runner is tagged out, the ball remains live and the interference is ignored.

Rule 7: Section 3: Article 5-Penalty, Page 45.

3. When the pitch is a third strike, the batter is out, the umpire can award a second out.

Rule 5: Section 1: DBT-Penalty 1, Page 37.

4. When there are two outs, the batter is out.

Rule 5: Section 1: DBT-Penalty 1, Page 37.

• The batter interferes while a runner is advancing home.

Exception: When the batter hits a throw from the pitcher who is not in contact with pitching plate, it's an immediate dead ball.

Rule 5: Section 1: DBT-Act. 2, Page 37.
Rule 5: Section 1: DBT-Act. 25, Page 37.

Results:

1. When runner is tagged out, the ball remains live and the interference is ignored.

Rule 5: Section 1: DBT-Penalty 2, Page 37.
Rule 7: Section 2: Article 5-Penalty, Page 45.

Ruling Continued on Page 62

2. When runner is not tagged out, time is called and the runner is called out.

> Rule 7: Section 2: Article 5-Penalty, Page 45.

Exception: When there are two outs, then the batter is out.

> Rule 5: Section 1: DBT-Penalty 2, Page 37.

- The umpire interferes with the catcher.

  Results:

  1. It is a delayed dead ball.

  > Rule 5: Section 1: DBT-Act. 8, Page 37.

  2. When the runner is not put out, all runners return.

  > Rule 5: Section 1: DBT-Penalty 8, Page 37.

Obstruction is a Delayed Dead Ball When:

- A catcher or fielder obstructs a batter.

    Rule 5: Section 1: DBT-Act. 3, Page 37.

    Result: When the batter and all runners attempting to steal or who are forced do not advance, award one base.

    Rule 5: Section 1: DBT-Award 3, Page 37.

- Runner being obstructed happens.

    Rule 5: Section 1: DBT-Act. 4, Page 37.

    Result: When an obstructed runner and all runners hindered by the obstruction do not reach bases they otherwise would have reached, award runner(s) the bases they were prevented from reaching.

    Rule 5: Section 1: DBT-Award 4, Page 37.

    Note: After the play has ended, it is the umpire's discretion to award bases that runners would have reached safely had the obstruction not occurred.

    Rule 2: Section 22: Article 1, Page. 21.
    Rule 8: Section 3: Article 2, Page. 52.

Pitched Ball is a Delayed Dead Ball When:

- The offensive team personnel calls "Time" or uses any other command or commits an act for the purpose of trying to cause a balk.

  Results:

  1. It is a delayed dead ball.

    Rule 5: Section 1: DBT-Act. 7, Page 37.

  2. No runners are allowed to advance, eject offender.

    Rule 5: Section 1: DBT-Penalty 7, Page 37.

- A batter deliberately removes his batting helmet in live ball territory while ball is live.

  Rule 5: Section 1: DBT-Act. 9, Page 37.

  Result: Team warning, next offender is ejected.

  Rule 5: Section 1: DBT-Penalty 9, Page 37.

Thrown Ball is a Delayed Dead Ball When:

• A defensive player intentionally touches a thrown ball, including a pitch, with detached player equipment.

Rule 5: Section 1: DBT-Act. 6, Page 37.

Result: Award two bases from the time of the infraction when base is not reached.

Rule 5: Section 1: DBT-Award 6, Page 37.

Deadball—Immediate

Batted Ball is an Immediate Dead Ball When:

- It is an illegally batted ball.

    Result: Batter is out, runners return.

    Rule 5: Section 1: DBT-Penalty 4, Page 36.

- A pitch is hit a second time.

    Result: Batter is out, runners return.

    Rule 5: Section 1: DBT-Penalty 5, Page 36.

- It is an uncaught foul ball.

    Result: Runners return to bases occupied at the time of the pitch.

Rule 5: Section 1: DBT-Penalty 6, Page 36.

Section Continued on Page 68

- A fair ball touches a spectator.

  Rule 5: Section 1: DBT-Act. 11, Page 36.

  Result: Award or penalize according to umpire's judgement.

  Rule 5: Section 1: DBT-Award or Penalty 11, Page 36.

- A fair ball does the following:

  1. Bounces over, through or lodges in fence.
  2. Lodges in player's uniform or equipment.

  Rule 5: Section 1: DBT-Act. 12, Page 36.

  Result: Award all runners two bases from base occupied at time of pitch.

  Rule 5: Section 1: DBT-Award 12, Page 36.

- A fair batted ball touches an umpire before it passes any fielder except the pitcher.

  Rule 5: Section 1: DBT-Act. 14, Page 36.

  Result: Runners return to bases occupied at the time of pitch unless forced by batter-runner. Batter awarded first.

  Rule 5: Section 1: DBT-Award 14, Page 36.

- A fair batted ball:

  1. Touches a runner before it touches an infielder.
  2. Passes any infielder except the pitcher and another fielder has a play.

  Rule 5: Section 1: DBT-Act. 13, Page 36.

  Results:

  a. The runner hit by the fair batted ball is out.
  b. The batter is awarded first base and credited with a single.

Ruling Continued on Page 69

   c. The runners return to the bases occupied at the time of the interference unless they are forced by the batter-runner.

Rule 5: Section 1: DBT-Penalty 13, Page 36.

- A fair or foul ball is caught while:

1. The fielder steps or falls with both feet over a barrier such as a fence, rope chalk line or pre-determined imaginary line.

Rule 5: Section 1: DBT-Act. 18.

2. The fielder steps or falls with both feet into a stand, bench or dugout.

Rule 5: Section 1: DBT-Act. 18, Page 36.

Result: Award all runners one base except when the caught ball is the third out.

Rule 5: Section 1: DBT-Award 18, Page 36.

- An infielder intentionally drops a fair fly, line drive or bunt in flight with at least first base occupied with less than two outs.

Rule 5: Section 1: DBT-Act. 19, Page 36.

Result: Batter is out and all runners return to base occupied at the time of pitch.

Rule 5: Section 1: DBT-Penalty 19, Page 36.

Batter Causes an Immediate Dead Ball When:

• A batter enters box with an illegal bat.

Rule 5: Section 1: DBT-Act. 23, Page 37.

Results:

1. Batter is out.
2. Coach is restricted to the dugout for the first offense.
3. Second offense coach is ejected.

Rule 5: Section 1: DBT-Penalty 23, Page 37.

• A batter refuses to enter box after being warned.

Rule 5: Section 1: DBT-Act. 24, Page 37.

Result: Strike is called.

Rule 5: Section 1: DBT-Penalty 24, Page 37.

• A batter contacts the catcher or his equipment prior to the pitch.

Rule 5: Section 1: DBT-Art. 28, Page 37.

Result: No penalty.

Rule 5: Section 1: DBT-Award 28, Page 37.

Defense is an Immediate Dead Ball When:

• There is defensive malicious contact.

Rule 5: Section 1: DBT-Act. 27, Page 37.

Result: Umpire will rule safe or out on the play and award runner(s) appropriate base(s) in his judgement.

Rule 5: Section 1: DBT-Award 27, Page 37.

Interference is an Immediate Dead Ball When:

- The runner or retired runner interferes with defense, including malicious contact.

Rule 5: Section 1: DBT-Act. 7, Page 36.

Result:

1. Interferer is out, when the interference prevented a double play at first, the batter-runner is also out.
2. Interferer is out, when the interference prevented a double play at a base other than first base, that runner would be called out.

Rule 5: Section 1: DBT-Penalty 7, Page 36.

- The offense interferes with a fielder attempting to catch a foul fly ball.

Rule 5: Section 1: DBT-Act. 8, Page 36.

Result: Runner is out and another runner is out when interference prevented a double play.

Rule 5: Section 1: DBT-Penalty 8, Page 36.

- Anyone on offensive team interferes with the defense.

Rule 5: Section 1: DBT-Act. 9, Page 36.

Result: The runner is out and other runner(s) return to bases occupied at the time of the interference.

Rule 5: Section 1: DBT-Penalty 9, Page 36.

- A home run ball is interfered with by a spectator or detached player equipment.

Rule 5: Section 1: DBT-Act. 10, Page 36.

Result: Award all runners home base.

Rule 5: Section 1: DBT-Award 10, Page 36

- The umpire interferes by:
  1. Handling a live ball.
  2. Calling time to inspect ball or for other reasons.
  3. Inadvertently calling foul.

Rule 5: Section 1: DBT-Act. 17, Page 36.

  Result: Runners return to bases they had reached or passed when ball became dead.

Rule 5: Section 1: DBT-Penalty 17, Page 36.

- A batted, thrown or pitched ball touches media area, anyone or thing that is entirely or practically in the media area.

Rule 5: Section 1: DBT-Act. 26, Page 37.

  1. Award runners one bases for a throw or pitch by the pitcher.
  2. Award runners two bases for a fair batted ball.
  3. Award runners two bases for any thrown ball except a pitcher in contact with the pitcher's plate.

Rule 5: Section 1: DBT-Award 26, Page 37.

Pitched Ball is an Immediate Dead Ball When:

• An intentional base on balls is awarded.

Rule 5: Section 1: DBT-Act. 22, Page 37.

Result: Batter is awarded first base.

Rule 5: Section 1: DBT-Award 22, Page 37.

• It's an illegal pitch with no runners.

Rule 5: Section 1: DBT-Act. 1, Page 36.

Result: The pitch is called a ball.

Rule 5: Section 1: DBT-Penalty 1, Page 36.

• The pitch touches a batter.

Rule 5: Section 1: DBT-Act. 2, Page 36.

Result: Batter is awarded first base except when he permits the ball to touch him or the pitch is a strike.

Rule 5: Section 1: DBT-Award 2, Page 36.

• The pitch touches a runner.

Rule 5: Section 1: DBT-Act. 3, Page 36.

Result: All runners advance one base, except when the pitch is a strike for third out.

Rule 5: Section 1: DBT-Award 3, Page 36.

• The pitcher is in contact with the pitching rubber a pitch and the pitch:
  1. Goes into the stands, benches, over / through a fence or backstop.
  2. Touches a spectator in live ball area.
  3. Lodges in catcher or umpire's equipment.

Rule 5: Section 1: DBT-Act. 16, Page 36.

Result: Award all runners one base.

Rule 5: Section 1: DBT-Award 16, Page 36.

- The pitch is a balk.

Rule 5: Section 1: DBT-Act. 20, Page 37.

Result: All runners advance one base. Batter remains at-bat.

Rule 5: Section 1: DBT-Award 20, Page 37.

- The umpire has given do not pitch signal.

Rule 5: Section 1: DBT-Act. 21, Page 37.

Result: No play can take place.

Rule 5: Section 1: DBT-Penalty 21, Page 37.

Thrown Ball is an Immediate Dead Ball When:

• Any player, other than the pitcher while in contact with the pitching rubber, throws a ball that goes into the bench or stands, or through or over a fence.

Rule 5: Section 1: DBT-Act. 15, Page 36.

Result: Award all runners two bases.

Rule 5: Section 1: DBT-Award 15, Page 36.

• A pitcher in contact with the pitching rubber throws to a base and the ball goes into the stand, bench, over or through fence, backstop, or touches a spectator in the live ball area or lodges in catcher or umpire's equipment.

Rule 5: Section 1: DBT-Act. 16, Page 36.

Result: Award all runners one base.

Rule 5: Section 1: DBT-Award 16, Page 36.

• A batter hits a throw from the pitcher (not in contact with pitcher's plate) while runner is coming home.

Rule 5: Section 1: DBT-Act. 25, Page 37.

Result: With less than two outs the runner is out, otherwise the batter is out.

Rule 5: Section 1: DBT-Penalty 25, Page 37.

Designated Hitter Rule

This chapter is relatively brief as the rulings pertaining to the designated hitter are pretty straightforward. The biggest twist for high school baseball concerning the designated hitter: any defensive play may have a designated hitter bat for them, not just the pitcher, as with many other levels of play.

Rulings for Designated Hitter

- A designated hitter must be stated on the initial lineup card.

  The use of a designated hitter is not allowed if it is not declared prior to beginning the game.

  Rule 3: Section 1: Article 4, Page 27.

- Any starting player not just the pitcher may have a designated hitter bat for them.

  The designated hitter can continue to bat for any substitutes for the original defensive player he was batting for.

  Rule 3: Section 1: Article 4, Page 27.

- Using a designated hitter creates a ten-man player lineup.

  The designated hitter cannot be a defensive player.

  Rule 3: Section 1: Article 4, Page 27.

- The designated hitter and any other starter can be substituted for, then re-enter the game once.

  When the designated hitter or a starter re-enters the game, he must re-enter in his original spot in the batting order.

  Rule 3: Section 1: Article 3, Page 27.

- When the designated hitter is pinch hit or pinch run for, that new player becomes the new designated hitter.

  Rule 3: Section 1: Article 4, Page 27.

- The designated hitter and the non-batting defensive player he is batting for are locked into the same batting spot in the batting order.

  Rule 3: Section 1: Article 4, Page 28.

The Designated Hitter is Terminated When:

- Any defensive player or previous defensive player who the designated hitter is batting for enters the game in any offensive capacity.

Rule 3: Section 1: Article 4-a, Page 28.

- Any designated hitter or previous designated hitter enters into the game defensively.

Rule 3: Section 1: Article 4-b, Page 28.

Infield Fly Rule in Effect

As with every chapter in this book, infield fly rule in effect rulings have been collected, converted into Basic English and listed in sequence and order of importance. The twist with this topic is the multiple numbers of variables where the "umpire's judgement" comes into play, depending upon where the infield fly lands, bounces, is hit, caught, dropped, or whether it is near a foul line. You can have converging players or a fly ball carrying out into the infield. Nothing is clear cut on an infield fly, so we offer insight on what to look out for and take into consideration that other rule books do not offer.

Definitions of an Infield Fly

- In order for an infield fly rule to be in effect, there has to be both of these:

  1. Less than two outs, with runners on first and second or runners on all bases.

  2. A ball that can be (not has to be) caught with ordinary effort by an infielder or outfielder.

    Rule 2: Section 19, Page 20.

- A line drive or an attempted bunt are not an infield fly.

    Rule 2: Section 19, Page 20.

- Once an infield fly rule is in effect, any defensive player can make the catch or not, and the batter-runner is out.

    Rule 2: Section 19, Page 20.

When the Infield Fly Rule is in Effect Rulings

- When a fly ball is first touched and caught runners must tag up.

Rule 8: Section 2: Article 5-Penalty, Page 47.

- While an infield fly rule is in effect, when the ball hits a runner who is in contact with a base, that runner is not out.

Rule 8: Section 4: Article 2-k-1, Page 55.

  Result: It is an immediate dead ball and the batter is out.

Rule 8: Section 4: Article 2-k-1, Page 55.

- With an infield fly rule in effect, the ball hits a runner who is not in contact with a base, both that runner and batter are out.

Rule 8: Section 4: Article 2-k-2, Page 55.

Author's Notes, Possible Infield Fly in Effect over Foul Line

- When an infield fly is landing near the foul line, the umpire will declare infield fly, "if fair".

  Rule 2: Section 19, Page 20.

  Author's note: It is very important to understand the five parameters that establishes a fair ball in order to correctly rule when an infield fly "if fair "is in effect. A fair batted ball must:

  1. Stop on fair ground between home to first base and home to third base.

     Rule 2: Section 4: Article 1-a, Page 16.

  2. Contact fair ground on or beyond an imaginary line between first and third base.

     Rule 2: Section 4: Article 1-b, Page 16.

  3. Be on or over fair ground while passing first or third base heading to the outfield.

     Rule 2: Section 41-c, Page 16.

  4. Land on fair ground on or beyond first or third base.

     Rule 2: Section 41-d, Page 16.

  5. Touch any base.

     Rule 2: Section 41-e, Page 16.

- With an Infield Fly rule in effect and the ball is landing near a foul line, an umpire must do these things before making a call:

  1. Point up at the ball.
  2. Verbally declare, "Infield Fly—If Fair!"
  3. Wait, to see where the ball will land and stop.

Ruling Continued on Page 85

4. Wait, to see when the ball is touched by the while over fair ground.

5. Then, make your call.

- An infield fly ball dropping near a foul line is dangerous because it can be caught, dropped, untouched over fair or foul territory. Or, bounce or roll in or out of either fair or foul territory.

- When an infield fly if fair is in effect dropping near a foul line, the following things can happen and the batter runner will be out:

  1. When the ball is touched or drops untouched and stays in fair territory.

  2. When the ball lands untouched hits a base then goes foul.

  3. When the ball lands untouched beyond an imaginary line that extends through first base and third base just behind the pitcher's plate in fair territory, then goes foul.

  4. When the ball lands foul then bounces back untouched into fair territory before first of third base and is either touched or stops fair.

- When an infield fly "if fair" is called:

  1. It is a foul ball and not an out when the ball lands in fair territory in front of an imaginary line between first and third base, then either bounces or rolls untouched and stops in foul territory.

  2. When the ball in foul territory is caught, it is an out.

Author's Notes, Infield Fly in Effect Summary

- Prior to calling infield fly, experienced umpires have been taught to observe the defense's actions in order to by rule establish ordinary effort.
  1. It may also be helpful to observe the base runners. Base runners' actions can also help indicate when you do or do not have an infield fly.
  2. When base runners are standing on or near their bases believing the ball will be caught, it is usually a strong indication you have an infield fly.
- Most fly balls can be caught with ordinary effort as long as the defensive player is in a proximity under the ball.
  1. By applying this logic even when the player is having trouble (wind) playing the ball or back peddling onto the grass, it is still possible to establish ordinary effort.
- A high towering fly ball falling inside the diamond with the infield fly criteria met;
  1. By putting the infield fly rule in effect, you are removing a force play on the runners on base.
  2. While runners are holding their bases believing the ball will be caught, understand that a non-call of an infield fly for whatever reason with the ball not being caught and stopping in fair ground, can easily result in a double or triple play.
  3. By calling the infield fly, the only penalty is the batter-runner is out.

Batter's Interference

Batter's interference has to be a good candidate for the least understood infractions in baseball. It seems that every time this infraction takes place and rulings are enforced, many players, coaches, or fans lose their minds. We have collected, organized, and listed rulings in sequence and order of importance so that you see every step needed to apply correct rulings. This is a play that, when you apply all the correct rulings, not only will coaches, players, and fans take notice, so will your umpiring peers.

Definition for Batter's Interference

- Definition of batter's interference is when the batter interferes with the catcher's fielding and throwing by:

    1. Leaning over home plate.

        Rule 7: Section 3: Article 5-a, Page 45.

    2. Stepping out of the batter's box.

        Rule 7: Section 3: Article 5-b, Page 45.

    3. Making any movement, including follow-through interference which hinders actions at home plate or the catcher's attempt to play on a runner.

        Rule 7: Section 3: Article 5-c, Page 45.

        Author's Note: Ruling number three articulates the majority of all Batter's Interference that would be called by stating "any movement", excluding ruling number four vacating a congested area.

    4. Not making a reasonable effort to vacate a congested area when there is a throw to home plate, while there was time for the batter to move away.

        Rule 7: Section 3: Article 5-d, Page 45.

Rulings for Batter's Interference

• When there are two outs, the batter is always out, no matter where a play may happen.

Rule 7: Section 3: Article 5-Penalty, Page 45.

• With less than two outs and the play is at first, second, or third base:

1. It is a delayed dead ball, let the play finish.

Rule 5: Section 1-Delayed Dead Ball Table-Activity 1, Page 37.

Rule 5: Section 1: Article 2-a, Page 38.

2. When the (attempt to put out a runner) is not successful:

Results:

a. It becomes an immediate dead ball.

Rule 5: Section 1: Article 2-a-1, Page 38.

b. The batter is called out.

Rule 7: Section 3: Article 5-Penalty, Page 45.

c. All runners return to bases occupied at the time of pitch.

Rule 7: Section 3: Article 5-Penalty, Page 45.

• After batter's interference and the initial attempt to put out the runner is not successful, no additional play is allowed.

Rule 5: Section 1: Article 2-a-1, Page 38.

• When the pitch is a third strike and in the umpire's judgment the batter's interference at any base or at home plate prevented a double play, additional outs can be ruled.

Rule 7: Section 3: Article 5-Penalty, Page 45.

Section Continued on Page 90

- When the attempt to put out a runner is successful, the batter's interference is ignored.

  Rule 7: Section 3: Article 5-Penalty, Page 45.

- When there is a play at home and less than two outs:
  1. The runner is always out, tagged or not.
  2. When the runner coming home is tagged out on the play:

     - The interference is ignored.
     - The ball remains live.

  3. When the runner coming home is not tagged out on the play:

     - Time is called.
     - The runner is called out.

       Rule 7: Section 3: Article 5-Penalty, Page 45.

Definition for Follow-Through Interference

• By definition follow-through interference is when the batter has swung at a pitch while his bat hits the catcher and:

1. Hinders the action at home plate.
2. Hinders the catcher's attempt to play at any base.

Rule 2: Section 21-4, Page 20.
Rule 7: Section 3: Article 5-c, Page 45.

Author's Note: All batter's interference rulings and penalties apply when batter's follow-through interference happens.

Examples:

a. The batter's follow-through swing hits the catcher while the runner from first is sliding into second.

Result: The batter is declared out, and the runner returns to base occupied at the time of the pitch.

Rule 7: Section 3: Article 5-c-Penalty, Page 45.
Rule 7: Section 3: Article 5-Penalty, Page 45.

b. The batter's strike three follow-through swing hits the catcher, causing him to drop the ball, while the runner who was on first is now half way to second base.

Ruling Continued on Page 92

Results:

1. Batter's interference.

> Rule 7: Section 3: Article 5-c, Page 45.

2. It is a delayed dead ball, but once an out does not result from the catcher's play it becomes an immediate dead ball.

> Rule 5: Section 1: Article 2-a, Page 38.
> Rule 5: Section 1: Article 2-a-1, Page 38.

3. A possible double play was prevented, both the batter and the runner are called out.

> Rule 7: Section 3: Article 5-Penalty, Page 45.

Definition for Backswing Interference

• By definition is when a batter contacts the catcher or his equipment prior to a pitch.

Rule 2: Section 21-5, Page 20.

Result: The ball is immediately dead.

Rule 7: Section 3: Article 7- Penalty, Page 45.
Rule 5: Section 1: Article 1-n, Page 38.

Interference Offense / Umpire / Spectator / Runner

Interference is one word that entails the possibility of any one of dozens of infractions caused by just about anyone in or around a baseball game. Umpires, coaches, spectators, base runners, and batters are all subject to interfering with live play intentionally or unintentionally, with a pitched ball, a batted ball, or thrown ball, verbally or physically, and it is up to the umpire to be aware of these dozens of infractions and apply the appropriate rulings. In this chapter, we have once again converted rule book language into basic English, collected, and put related infractions and rulings together so that it is not only easier to find, but easier to study, retain, and apply.

Definition for Offensive Interference

- The team batting verbally or physically obstructs, impedes, hinders or confuses any fielder attempting to make a play.

Rule 2: Section 21-1-a, Page 20.

- The runner creates malicious contact while any defensive fielder:

    1. When the defensive player holds or does not hold the ball.
    2. While the defensive player is either in or out of the baseline.

Rule 2: Section 21-1-b, Page 20.

Rulings for Offensive Interference

- Any runner interferes with a throw, thrown ball or hinders a fielder's initial attempt to field a batted ball that runner is out.

  Rule 8: Section 4: Article 2-g, Page 54.
  Rule 5: Section 1-Dead Ball Table, Penalty 7, Page 36.

  Results:

  1. It is an immediate dead ball.

  Rule 5: Section 1-Dead Ball Table, Activity 7, Page 36.

  2. All other runners return to bases occupied at the time of the interference.

  Rule 8: Section 2: Article 9, Page 49.

  Notes:

  1. When either a retired runner or any other runner interferes and prevents a secondary out, that second out will be called by the umpire.

  2. When the umpire is unsure who the second player who would have been played on is, the player closest to home will be called out.

  Rule 8: Section 4: Article 2-g, Page 54 & 55.

- One player or coach may occupy each coaching box.

  Rule 3: Section 2: Article 1, Page 28.

- No other player shall be near a base or baseline a runner is trying to reach, in attempting to draw a throw or confuse the defense.

  Rule 3: Section 2: Article 3, Page 28.

Ruling Continued on Page 98

Results:

1. It is an immediate dead ball.

> Rule 5: Section 1-Dead Ball Table, Activity 9, Page 36.
> Rule 3: Section 2: Article 3-Penalty, Page 29.

2. The runner will be called out.

> Rule 3: Section 2: Article 3-Penalty, Page 29.
> Rule 5: Section 1-Dead Ball Table, Penalty 9, Page 36.

3. All other runners return to bases occupied at the time of the interference.

> Rule 8: Section 6: Article 9, Page 49.
> Rule 3: Section 2: Article 3-Penalty, Page 29.

- When an offensive team member including the base coach fail to vacate any area needed by the defense attempting to put out the runner or batter.

> Rule 3: Section 2: Article 3, Page 28.

Results:

1. It is an immediate dead ball.

> Rule 5: Section 1-Dead Ball Table, Activity 9, Page 36.
> Rule 3: Section 2: Article 3-Penalty, Page 29.

2. The runner will be called out.

> Rule 3: Section 2: Article 3-Penalty, Page 29.
> Rule 5: Section 1-Dead Ball Table, Penalty 9, Page 36.

3. All other runners return to bases occupied at the time of the interference.

> Rule 8: Section 2: Article 9, Page 49.
> Rule 3: Section 2: Article 3-Penalty, Page 29.

Rulings for Runner Interference

- The runner is out when he creates malicious contact with any fielder, with or without the ball, in or out of the baseline.

  Rule 2: Section 21-1-b, Page 20.

  Note: Malicious contact supersedes obstruction.

  Rule 8: Section 4: Article 2-e-1, Page 54.

- When any offensive team member (excluding runners) interferes with a defensive player attempting to field a foul fly ball the batter is out.

  Rule 7: Section 4-f, Page 46.

  Results:
  1. It is an immediate dead ball.

     Rule 5: Section 1-Dead Ball Table, Activity 9, Page 36.

  2. All other runners return to bases occupied at the time of the interference.

     Rule 5: Section 1-Dead Ball Table, Penalty 9, Page 36

- When the interference prevented a double play in the umpire's judgement, two outs will be called.

  Rule 8: Section 4: Article 2-g, Page 54, 55.

- When the defensive player misplays the initial play then moves less than a step and a reach going after the ball and contact is made, the runner is still out for interference.

  Rule 8: Section 4: Article 2-g, Page 54

Section Continued on Page 100

- When the defensive player misplays the initial play then moves beyond a step and a reach going after the ball while the (runner is contacted or path altered), that defensive player is then obstructing the runner.

Rule 8: Section 4: Article 2-g, Page 54.

- When the runner intentionally makes contact while the defensive player is beyond a step and a reach when fielding a misplayed ball, it would still be runner's interference.

Rule 8: Section 4: Article 2-g Page 54.

Author's Note: Step and a reach is a parameter that defines the defensive player's area of protection from interference while attempting to field a misplayed ball. Beyond this area the defensive player's protection from interference ends, and the runner's protection from obstruction begins.

Malicious Contact by a Runner

- When a runner creates malicious contact with any fielder, with or without the ball, in or out of the baseline.

  Results:

  1. Penalty for offensive malicious contact is ejection.
     Rule 3: Section 3: Article 1-m-Penalty, Page 30.

  2. It is an immediate dead ball.
     Rule 3: Section 3: Article 1-m-Penalty, Page30.

  Note: Malicious contact supersedes obstruction.
  Rule 8: Section 4: Article 2-e-1, Page 54.

- When the player scores before his malicious contact happens, the run counts and he is ejected.
  Rule 3: Section 3: Article 1-m-Penalty, Page 30.

- When the player does not score before his malicious contact happens, that player is called out and ejected.
  Rule 3: Section 3: Article 1-m-Penalty, Page 30.

- Runners are awarded appropriate bases per umpire's judgement.
  Rule 8: Section 4: Article 2-e-1, Page 54.

Author's Notes Malicious Contact

- You may have malicious contact when:
  1. The offending player intentionally applied excessive force.
  2. The offending player's contact was applied above the waist to the other player.
  3. The offending player's contact, did violently remove or harm the other player.

Section Continued on Page 102

- Lowered shoulders, raised elbows and forearms are all strong indicators when you have malicious contact.

- The receiving player's physical condition after contact is another strong indicator when you have malicious contact.

    Example: Receiving players of malicious contact frequently will remain lying at or near the point of contact in an obvious state of confusion, pain and inability to continue play.

- The majority of violent (malicious contact) collisions happen at home plate.

- Runners must slide or avoid making contact, malicious or not with any defensive player.

- Either offensive or defensive players can be penalized for malicious contact.

Umpire's Interference When:

• The umpire hinders, impedes or prevents a catcher's attempt to throw.

Rule 2: Section 21-2, Page 20.

Results:

1. Delayed dead ball, let the play finish.

Rule 5: Section 1: Dead Ball Table, Activity 8, Page 37.

2. When the runner is not put out he and all runners return to their bases at the time of the interference.

Rule 8: Section 3: Article 6, Page 52 & 53.

• A fair batted ball touches an umpire before touching any fielder and before passing any infielder excluding the pitcher.

Rule 2: Section 21-2, Page 20.
Rule 5: Section 1: Dead Ball Table-Activity-14, Page 36.

Results:

1. It is an immediate dead ball.

2. Batter is awarded first base.

3. Runners return to bases occupied at the time of the pitch, unless forced.

Rule 5: Section 1: Dead Ball Table, Activity 14, Page 36.

• A ball either pitched or thrown by the pitcher while in contact with the pitcher's plate that lodges in umpire's equipment.

Rule 5: Section 1-g-4, Page 38.
Rule 5: Section 1: Activity 16-Dead Ball Table, Page 36.

Results:

1. It is an immediate dead ball.

2. Award all runners one base.

Rule 5: Section 1: Dead Ball Table, Activity 16, Page 36.

It is Not Umpire's Interference When:

- A base umpire runs or bumps into a base-runner causing the runner to trip, stumble, or fall.

    Result: Live play continues.

- The catcher drops a pitched ball that is then kicked away from the defense by the plate umpire allowing a run to score.

    Result: Live play continues and the run scores.

Author's Note: To the best of my knowledge, the above statements are not in the official NFHS rule or case books, yet both can and do happen in baseball games.

Spectator's Interference When:

- The spectator impedes the progress of a game.

Rule 2: Section 21-3, Page 19.

Results:

1. It is an immediate dead ball.
2. Bases will be awarded according to umpire judgement that would offset the spectator interference.

Rule 5: Section 1: Dead Ball Table-Activity 11, Page 36.
Rule 8: Section 3: Article 3-e, Page 52.

Coach's Interference When:

• They physically assist runner during playing action.

Rule 3: Section 2: Article 2, Page 28.

Result: Assisted runner is immediately out.

Rule 3: Section 2: Article 2-Penalty, Page 27.
Rule 8: Section 4: Article 2-s, Page 56.

• They intentionally interfere in fair territory or with a thrown ball.

Rule 3: Section 2: Article 3, Page 28 & 29.

Results:

1. The ball becomes dead immediately.

Rule 5: Section 1: Dead Ball Table-Activity 9, Page 36.

2. The runner is out.

Rule 3: Section 2: Article 3-Penalty, Page 29.
Rule 5: Section 1: Dead Ball Table-Act-Penalty 9, Page 36.

3. All other runners return to bases occupied at the time of the interference.

Rule 8: Section 2: Article 9, Page 49.

Obstruction

Obstruction in baseball is many things. It can be extremely obvious, as when a runner is physically knocked to the ground while running the bases. It can be as subtle as an infielder brushing the arm of a base runner. In all cases, knowing what to do is extremely important. With just about every live batted ball, when infractions take place, everyone is excited, noise elevates, and confusion can overcome many. Obstruction is no exception. Teams and fans immediately want the umpire to intervene and can't understand why he is allowing play to continue. This chapter provides the answer and much more in a format that, when studied, can be retained and correctly applied while others are frantic and confused.

Definition of Obstruction

- Any act by any member of the defensive team, including a catcher or fielder, hindering a batter or runner that is intentional or unintentional, verbal or physical, or that changes the pattern of the play.

Rule 2: Section 22-1, Page 21.

Notes:

1. It is also obstruction when a defensive player without the ball prevents the runner access to a base that he is trying to attain.

Rule 2: Section 22-3, Page 21.

2. A simulated tag without the ball (fake tag) is obstruction.

Rule 2: Section 22-2 Page 21.

Obstructed Runner:

• It is a delayed dead ball. Let the play finish.

Rule 2: Section 22-1, Page 21.
Rule 5: Section 1-Delayed Dead Ball Table Activity 4, Page 37.

Base Awards:

1. The runner who is obstructed while advancing or returning will be awarded one additional base from the spot where the obstruction occurred.

2. All runners includving the obstructed runner will be awarded additional bases they would have reached when the obstruction had not happened.

Rule 8: Section 3: Article 2, Page 51.

• After the play has ended, a one-base minimum will be awarded. It is the umpire's judgment to award additional bases that the runners would have reached safely had the obstruction not occurred.

Example: When a runner is obstructed going to second base, but is thrown out continuing to third base the umpire can rule him safe when the umpire determines the obstruction caused the runner to be out.

Rule 2: Section 22: Article 1, Page. 21.
Rule 8: Section 3: Article 2, Page. 51

Section Continued on Page 110

- Additional base awards supersede obstruction base awards.

Rule 8: Section 3: Article 2 Page 51.

Example: A batted ball thrown by an outfielder goes out of play after obstruction has happened, all runners would be awarded two bases from the time of throw.

Rule 8: Section 3: Article 2 Page 51.

Exception: Malicious contact supersedes obstruction.

Rule 8: Section 4: Article 2-e-1, Page 54.

Malicious Contact Supersedes Obstructed Runner

- Malicious contact supersedes obstruction.

Rule 8: Section 4: Article 2-e-1, Page 54.

Example: When the defense is in the runner's base path and the runner initiates malicious contact, obstruction is ignored.

Rule 8: Section 4: Article 2-e-1, Page 54.

Results:

1. The offender will be ejected.

Rule 3: Section 3: Article 1-Penalty-m, Page 30.

2. The runner is out when he creates malicious contact with any fielder, with or without the ball, in or out of the baseline.

Rule 2: Section 21: Article 1-b, Page 20.

- When the runner scores before his malicious contact happens, the run counts and he is ejected.

Rule 3: Section 3: Article 1-m-Penalty, Page 30.

- When the runner does not score before his malicious contact happens, that player is called out and ejected.

Rule 3: Section 3: Article 1-m-Penalty, Page 30.

Author's Notes Malicious Contact

- You may have malicious contact when:
  1. The offending player intentionally applied excessive force.
  2. The offending player's contact was applied above the waist to the other player.
  3. The offending player's contact, did violently remove or harm the other player.

Section Continued on Page 112

- Lowered shoulders, raised elbows and forearms are all strong indicators when you have malicious contact.

- The receiving player's physical condition after contact is another strong indicator when you have malicious contact.

- Example: Receiving players of malicious contact frequently will remain lying at or near the point of contact in an obvious state of confusion, pain and inability to continue play.

- The majority of violent (malicious contact) collisions happen at home plate.

- Runners must slide or avoid making contact, malicious or not with any defensive player.

- Either offensive or defensive players can be penalized for malicious contact.

Obstructed Batter

- Once a batter is obstructed by the defense (usually the catcher) he is then considered a runner.

Rule 8: Section 1: Article 1-e, Page 46.

Results:

1. It is a delayed dead ball, let the play finish.

Rule 2: Section 22-1, Page 21.
Rule 5: Section 1: Delayed Dead Ball Table Activity 3, Page 37.

2. All runners who are stealing or forced are awarded one base when a defensive player (usually the catcher) obstructs the batter by:

   a. Catcher stepping on or across home plate.

   b. Catcher pushing the batter to reach for a pitch.

   c. Catcher touching the bat.

Rule 8: Section 3: Article 1-c, Page 51.

   Exception: When a runner is not stealing or forced, they will not be awarded one base.

Rule 8: Section 1: Article 1-e-1, Page 47.

- Any runners attempting to advance during a steal or a squeeze play while the batter is obstructed, shall be awarded that base.

Rule 8: Section 1: Article 1-e-1, Page 47.

- Runners who are not forced or stealing when a batter has been obstructed, must return to their base at the time of the pitch.

Rule 8: Section 1: Article 1-e-1, Page 47.

Section Continued on Page 114.

- When the batter is obstructed, the offense has the option to decline the defensive player's (usually catcher's) obstruction base award and accept the final outcome of the play.

Rule 8: Section 1: Article 1-e, Page 46, 47.

Results:

1. It is a delayed dead ball, let the play finish.

Rule 5: Section 1: Dead Ball Table, Activity-3, Page 37.

2. When the obstructed batter or runners attempting to steal or who are forced do not advance, they will be awarded one base.

Rule 5: Section 1: Dead Ball Table, Penalty-3, Page 37.

Note: Option to decline or accept outcome of the play will happen before:

a. The next legal or illegal pitch.

b. An intentional walk.

c. The infielders leave the diamond.

Rule 8: Section 1: Article 1-e Page 46, 47.

Exception: The obstruction is ignored when the batter-runner reaches first and all other runners advance one base.

Rule 8: Section 1: Article 1-e Page 46, 47.

Author's Notes, Obstruction

- In high school baseball it is considered obstruction when the catcher makes contact with the batter or bat while the batter is swinging at a pitch, it is not considered interference.

- In high school baseball there is only one type of obstruction, whether a play is being made on the obstructed runner, batter, batter-runner or not.

Pitching Positions, Stances & Substitutions

With only two positions for the pitcher to begin pitching from, this should be a simple and easy topic to cover. Quite the opposite is true, because after the pitcher establishes which of the two positions he will pitch from, just about every element of the pitcher's body is restricted or required to do or not do specific actions. The pitcher's defensive actions are regulated more heavily than any other defensive player.

Both Set and Windup Positions, Rulings

- Pitching regulations begin when the pitcher intentionally contacts the pitcher's plate.

  Rule 6: Section 1: Article 1, Page 39.

- The pitcher will:
  1. Face the batter in either the set or windup position.
  2. Take his sign from the catcher with his pivot foot in contact with the pitcher's plate.

  Rule 6: Section 1: Article 1, Page 39.

- The position of the pitcher's feet will determine when he will pitch from the set or windup position.

  Rule 6: Section 1: Article 1, Page 39.

- When the pitcher make an illegal act while in contact with the pitcher's plate during his set or wind-up position, then:
  1. It is an immediate dead ball.
  2. It is a balk with runners on base.
  3. A (ball is awarded to the batter) with no runners on base.

  Rule 6: Section 1: Article 1, 2, 3-Penalty, Page 40.

Legal Set Stance Illustrated

- The pivot foot is in contact and parallel with the pitcher's plate.

  Rule 6: Section 1: Article 3, Page 40.

- It is legal for both feet to be outside the outer edges of the pitcher's plate in the set position.

Legal Windup Stance Illustrated

• The pivot foot is in contact with the pitcher's plate.

Rule 6: Section 1: Article 1, Page 39.

• The non-pivot foot is on or behind a line extending outward from the front edge of the pitcher's plate.

Rule 6: Section 1: Article 2, Page 40.

Illegal Windup Stance Illustrated

- The non-pivot foot is not on or behind a line extending across, outward from and parallel with the front edge of the pitcher's plate.

Rule 6: Section 1: Article 2, Page 40.

Set Position, Rulings

- The pitcher's entire non-pivot foot will be in front of a line extending outward from and parallel with the front edge of the pitcher's plate.

- The ball may be in either his hand or glove.

- His pitching hand can be down at his side or behind his back.

Rule 6: Section 1: Article 3, Page 40.

Windup Position, Rulings

• The pitcher's pivot foot will be in contact with the pitcher's plate.

Rule 6: Section 1: Article 1 Page 39.

• The pitcher's non-pivot foot shall be in any position on or behind a line extending across, outward from and parallel with the front edge of the pitcher's plate.

Rule 6: Section 1: Article 2, Page 40.

• There are no restrictions on how the pitcher holds the ball. Position of hands include:

1. Together in front of his body.
2. Both hands at his side.
3. Either hand in front or at his side.

Rule 6: Section 1: Article 2, Page 40.

Both Set and Windup Positions, Summary

- In the set position the pitcher's pivot foot will be in contact with and parallel with the front edge of the pitcher's plate.

Rule 6: Section 1: Article 3, Page 40.

- In the windup position the non-pivot foot can be anywhere on or behind the line extending across, outward from and parallel with the front edge of the pitcher's plate.

Rule 6: Section 1: Article 2, Page 40.

Pitching Substitutions

- The starting pitcher must pitch until the first opposing batter has been put out or has advanced to a base.

Rule 3: Section 1: Article 1, Page 26.

Result: When the starting pitcher does not face one batter, he can play another defensive position, but cannot return to pitch.

Rule 3: Section 1: Article 1-Penalty, Page 26.

- When a pitcher is replaced while his team is on defense, the new substitute pitcher must pitch to the batter who is then at-bat or any substitute for that-batter until:

1. That-batter is put out.
2. Reaches a base.
3. The third out is made.

Rule 6: Section 1: Article 2, Page 27.

Results:

  a. A charged conference that would violate the above rule will be denied.
  b. When the pitcher is injured or ejected, the above rules are ignored.

Rule 6: Section 1: Article 2, Page 27\

Section Continued on Page 124

- A pitcher may be removed and go to another defensive position, then return as pitcher only once per inning provided his return does not violate:

  1. The pitching rule.

     Rule 3: Section 1: Article 2, Page 27.
     Rule 3: Section 1: Article 1, Page 26.

  2. The substitution rule.

     Rule 3: Section 1: Article 2, Page 27

  3. Charged conference rule.

     Rule 3: Section 1: Article 2, Page 27.
     Rule 3: Section 4: Article 1, Page 31.

- A starting pitcher after leaving the game can re-enter like any other starter, but not as pitcher.

  Rule 3: Section 1: Article 3, Page 27.

- He cannot return to pitch from another defensive position in the same inning when:

  1. He was removed for an injury.

  2. Did not finish throwing to the first batter until he was out or reached a base.

  3. His replacement requires more warm-up throws than permitted.

     Rule 3: Section 1: Article 2, Page 27.

Runner, Run Lane & Slide Rulings

Batter-runner and base-runners are constantly under the watchful eyes of the umpires for many reasons. Similar to the pitcher on defense, runners are closely regulated in what they can and cannot do during live-ball play. Where they run, when they run, where they slide, how they slide, avoiding the ball, and avoiding the defense are all discussed in this chapter. Again, we have collected and listed similar rulings together making finding them, studying them, and retaining them not only easier but more effective.

Runner Hit by a Fair Batted Ball Rulings:

- The runner is out when a fair batted ball hits him before:
1. It touches an infielder.
2. It passes an infielder, excluding the pitcher.

The batted ball can pass the pitcher then strike the runner and that runner is still out. Only for the purpose of this rule the pitcher while disengaged from the pitcher's plate is not considered an infielder.

Rule 8: Section 4: Article 2-k. Page 55.
Rule 6: Section 1: Article 5, Page 41.

Results:
1. It is an immediate dead ball.

Rule 5: Section 1: Dead ball Table, Activity 13, Page 36.

2. Batter is awarded first base and all other runners return to bases occupied at the time of the interference, unless forced.

Rule 5: Section 1: Dead Ball Table, Award-Penalty 13, Page 36.

Exception: After the batted ball has passed, not touching an infielder, the ball then strikes a runner and when the umpire is convinced that a secondary back up fielder could have made a play, that runner is out.

Rule 8: Section 4: Article 2-k, Page 55.

Runner Hit by Fair Fly Ball, While Infield Fly Rule is in Effect Rulings:

• The runner is in contact with a base and is hit by the infield fly they are not out.

> Result: It is an immediate dead ball.
>
> Rule 8: Section 4: Article 2-k-1, Page 55.

• The runner is off a base and is hit by an infield fly ball, both the hit runner and batter would be out.

> Rule 8: Section 4: Article 2-k-2, Page 55.

> Result: It is an immediate dead ball.
>
> Rule 8: Section 4: Article 2-k-1, Page 55.

• A runner does not have to vacate his base to permit a fielder to catch a fly ball, but he cannot interfere.

> Rule 8: Section 2: Article 8, Page 49.

Two Runners Occupy the Same Base Rulings:

• When both runners are tagged the trail runner is out.

Rule 8: Section 2: Article 8, Page 49.

• With two runners on the same base, when the base or runners are tagged, the trail runner is called out.

Rule 8: Section 2: Article 8-a, Page 49.

Trail Runner Passes Lead Runner Rulings:

* As soon as the trail runner passes the lead runner the trail runner is out.

> Rule 8: Section 4: Article 2-m, Page 55.

Result: The ball stays live. This is the same ruling as when a base coach assists a runner.

> Rule 3: Section 2: Article 2-Penalty, Page 27.
> Rule 8: Section 4: Article 2-s, Page 56.

Note: The lead runner is no longer forced to run when the runner who follows him is called out, or as in the case of this rule after he is passed by the trail runner.

> Rule 8: Section 4: Article 2-j-1, Page 55.

Runner Returns to Touch Missed Base or Tag Up Rulings:

- A runner returning to touch a missed base or a base left early while tagging up, will retouch bases in reverse order.

  Rule 8: Section 2: Article 2, Page 47.

- Any runner who has missed a base may not retouch it, when a trailing runner has scored.

  Rule 8: Section 2: Article 3, Page 47.

- Runners returning to touch a missed base or a base they left early while tagging up must do so immediately.

  Rule 8: Section 2: Article 5, Page 47.

- Runner returning to tag a base can be put out by being tagged or by touching the base before the runner does.

  Rule 8: Section 2: Article 6-k, Page 48.

  Exception: When the batter-runner safely touches first base and then runs or slides past the bag, he can return to the bag without penalty of being put out.

  Rule 8: Section 4: Article 2-h-1, Page 55.

  Exceptions to the Exception:
  1. When the batter-runner was awarded a base on balls he is still is at risk for being tagged out for leaving his bag.
  2. When the batter-runner safely touches first base and then runs or slides past the bag and then feints or runs towards second base, he can be tagged out prior to retuning to a base.

     Rule 8: Section 4: Article 2-h-1, Page 55.

A Player Cannot Return to a Missed Base
or to Tag Up Rulings:

- A runner may not return to tag a missed base or for leaving early while tagging up on a fly ball when:
    1. The ball becomes dead.

        Rule 8: Section 2: Article 6-d-1, Page 48.
    2. The runner has left the field of play.

        Rule 8: Section 2: Article 6-d-2, Page 48.
    3. A trailing runner has scored.

        Rule 8: Section 2: Article 6-d-3, Page 48.
    4. The ball becomes dead while the runner is on or beyond a succeeding base and a legal appeal is made.

        Rule 8: Section 4: Article 2-q, Page 56.

Runner's Path Between Bases Rulings:

- While the defense is attempting to tag the runner, he is out when he moves beyond three feet from a direct line between bases.

Rule 8: Section 4: Article 2-a, Page 54.

  Exception: The runner is not out when the batted ball is in the runner's path and the runner goes behind the fielder to avoid interfering.

Rule 8: Section 4: Article 2-a-1, Page 54.

- A runner establishes a new (imaginary) base line between his location and the base he is going with every play made on him.

Rule 8: Section 4: Article 2-a-2, Page 54.

Three Foot Running Lane Rulings:

The batter-runner is out when:

- The batter-runner steps outside the three-foot running lane with an entire foot during the last half of the distance from home plate to first base, and he interferes with a fielder or throw.

Rule 8: Section 4: Article 1-g, Page 53.
Rule 8: Section 4: Article 1-g-2, Page 53.

> Note: Running and stepping outside the three-foot running lane is ignored when:
>
> 1. It is to avoid a fielder attempting to field a batted ball.
> 2. The batter-runner does not interfere with a fielder or a throw.

Rule 8: Section 4: Article 1-g-1, Page 53.

Legal Slide Rulings:

- Head first.

  Rule 2: Section 32-1, Page 24.

- Feet first, one leg and buttock on ground.

  Rule 2: Section 32-1, Page 24.

- Runner must be in reach of the base with either a hand or foot.

  Rule 2: Section 32-1, Page 24.

- Runner can legally slide or run away from defensive player to avoid contact or altering the play.

  Rule 2: Section 32-1, Page 24.

- Slide beyond home plate (baseline extended) and make non-malicious contact or alter the play.

  Rule 2: Section 32-2-c, Page 24.

- Runners are never required to slide.
  1. Jumping, hurdling, and leaping are all legal attempts to avoid a fielder as long as the fielder is lying on the ground.
  2. Diving over the fielder is illegal.

  Rule 8: Section 4: Article 2-b-2, Page 54.

Illegal Slide Rulings:

Runner is out when he does the following:

- Rolls, cross-body or pops up into a defensive player.

  Rule 2: Section 32-2-a, Page 24.

- Raises his leg higher than fielder's knee, when fielder is in a standing position.

  Rule 2: Section 32-2-b, Page 24.

- Slides beyond first, second or third base and makes contact or alters the play.

  Rule 2: Section 32-2-c, Page 24.

- Slashes or kicks a defensive player.

  Rule 2: Section 32-2-d, Page 24.

- Tries to injure defensive player.

  Rule 2: Section 32-2-e, Page 24.

- On a force play does not slide on the ground in a direct line between bases.

  Rule 2: Section 32-2-f, Page 23.

  Exception: Runner can slide away or runaway from a defensive player.

  Rule 2: Section 32-1, Page 24.
  Rule 8: Section 4: Article 2-b-1, Page 54.

- Diving over the fielder is illegal.

  Rule 8: Section 4: Article 2-b-2, Page 54.

- He does not legally slide and causes illegal contact.

  Rule 8: Section 4: Article 2-b, Page 54.

- He illegally alters the actions of a fielder making a play.

  Rule 8: Section 4: Article 2-b, Page 54.

- He does not slide in a direct line between bases.

  Rule 8: Section 4: Article 2-b, Page 54.

Force Play Slide Rulings:

• When a runner is forced to run and a play is being made on him he must do one of these three things:

1. Slide in a direct line between bases.

Rule 8: Section 4: Article 2-b, Page 54.

2. Slide away from the defense and avoid contact or altering the play.

Rule 8: Section 4: Article 2-b-1, Page 54.

3. Run away from the area of play, avoid contact or altering the play.

Rule 8: Section 4: Article 2-b-2, Page 54.

Substitutions and Courtesy Runner

Knowing when a player can enter the game or re-enter the game is never as easy as it may seem. Is the player eligible? Is the player a courtesy runner, or has he already been in the game? These are reasonable questions for which the umpire must provide the correct rulings. In this chapter, we have collected and converted these rulings into basic English so that when a player enters, a player re-enters, or a courtesy runner enters the game, you will know what to do and rule accordingly.

Definition of Eligible Substitute

- An eligible substitute can replace any player in the lineup.

Rule 2: Section: Article 36-1, Page 24, 25.

- An unreported eligible substitute can legally enter the game without reporting in. No penalty!

Rule 2: Section: Article 36-2, Page 24, 25.

Illegal Substitute, Rulings

• Is a player who enters or re-enters the game without eligibility to do so.

> Rule 2: Section 36: Article 3-a, Page 25.

> Penalty: Upon discovery of an illegal substitute, they are called out and restricted to the bench or dugout for the remainder of the game.

> Rule 3: Section 1: Article 1, Page 26.

• Is a player who re-enters game in wrong position in the batting order.

> Rule 2: Section 36: Article 3-b, Page 25.

> Penalty: Upon discovery of an illegal substitute, they are called out and restricted to the bench or dugout for the remainder of the game.

> Rule 3: Section 1: Article 1, Page 26.

• Is a player who enters on defense while the player for whom he is batting is also in on defense.

> Rule 2: Section 36: Article 3-c, Page 25.

> Penalty: Upon discovery of an illegal substitute, they are called out and restricted to the bench or dugout for the remainder of the game.

> Rule 3: Section 1: Article 1, Page 26.

• A substitute who is removed from the game cannot re-enter. Only starters may re-enter.

> Rule 3: Section 1: Article 3, Page 27.

> Penalty: Upon discovery of an illegal substitute, they are called out and restricted to the bench or dugout for the remainder of the game.

> Rule 3: Section 1: Article 1, Page 26.

Section Continued on Page 140

- When the defensive player for whom the designated hitter is batting for enters in a different spot in the batting order as a batter or runner.

Rule 2: Section 36: Article 3-d, Page 25.
Rule 3: Section 1: Article 3, Page 26.

Penalty: Upon discovery of an illegal substitute, they are called out and restricted to the bench or dugout for the remainder of the game.

Rule 3: Section 1: Article 1, Page 26.

- A player who violates the courtesy runner rule.

Rule 2: Section 36: Article 3-e, Page 25.
Courtesy Runners, Page 65.

Penalty: Upon discovery of an illegal substitute, they are called out and restricted to the bench or dugout for the remainder of the game.

Rule 3: Section 1: Article 1, Page 26.

Courtesy Runner-Speed Up Rules

- Offense can use a courtesy runner at any time for either the pitcher and or the catcher.

Speed-up Rule 1, Page 65.

1. A courtesy runner does not change the batting order.

Speed-up Rule 1, Page 65.

- The same player may not be used as a courtesy runner for both the pitcher and catcher.

Speed-up Rule 2, Page 65.

- The pitcher or catcher are not removed from the lineup when a courtesy runner is used.

Speed-up Rule 3, Page 65.

- Any player who has been in the game in any capacity is not eligible to be a courtesy runner.

Speed-up Rule 4, Page 65.

- When a courtesy runner enters the game, he cannot re-enter into the game as a substitute in that same half inning.

Speed-up Rule 5, Page 65.

  Exception: The courtesy runner can be used as a substitute in the same half inning when no other runners are available during an injury, illness or ejection.

Speed-up Rule 5, Page 65.

- The umpire-in-chief records courtesy runners and informs the scorekeeper.

Speed-up Rule 6, Page 6.

Section Continued on Page 142

- An illegal courtesy runner is considered an illegal substitute.

Speed-up Rule 7, Page 65.

Result: An illegal courtesy runner shall be called out and restricted to bench/dugout for remainder of game.

Rule 2: Section 36: Article 3-e, Page 24, 25.
Rule 3: Section 1: Article 1, Page 26.

- Should a courtesy runner become ill, injured or ejected, another eligible courtesy runner can replace him.

Speed-up Rule 7, Page 65.

- The umpire or either team may disclose an illegal courtesy runner.

Rule 3: Section 1: Article 1, Page 26.

Verbal and Written Warnings— Ejections

You know that every game is not going to be problem-free. You know that not all coaches will be understanding or good sports when things go wrong. You know the players and fans are going to test the limits of what you, as an umpire, are willing to accept or ignore. Knowing all these potentially problematic scenarios can show up at any given moment during a baseball game, we have provided information in this chapter that can prepare you to intervene before a small problem becomes a huge problem. Resolving these issues before they balloon into disaster should be your priority; waiting and believing they will go away or resolve on their own is where the real problems start.

Verbal and Written Warnings—Ejections

- First minor offense the offender will receive a verbal or written warning.

Rule 3: Section 3: Article 1-Penalty, Page 29.
Rule 3: Section 3: Article 1-f through k, Penalty, 29, 30.

1. When the first offense is egregious enough, the offender can be ejected.

Rule 3: Section 3: Article 1-f through k, Penalty, Page 29, 30.

- Second minor offense the offender receives a written warning and they are restricted to the bench/dugout for the remainder of the game.

Rule 3: Section 3: Article 1-f through k, Penalty, Page 29, 30.

Example of a minor offense: Any member of the coaching staff who is not the head coach leaves the dugout or coaching box to dispute a judgement call.

Rule 3: Section 3: Article 1-f-6, Page 29.

Exception: When the offense is severe enough the umpire can eject just the offending coach, while keeping the head coach on the bench or eject both.

Rule 3: Section 3: Article 1-f-6-Penalty, Page 30.

- When a coach receives a written warning, they are restricted to the bench or dugout for the remainder of the game.

Rule 3: Section 3: Article 1-f – k, Penalty, Page 29, 30.

- A coach after receiving a written warning, will be ejected for any additional offenses.

Rule 3: Section 3: Article 1-f – k, Penalty, Page 29, 30.

- Officials will keep and record all warnings.

Rule 10: Section 2: Article 3-j, Page 64

- Major offenses the offender will be ejected.

  Rule 3: Section 3: Article 1-l-q-Penalty, Page 30.

  Example of a major offense: Physical contact, spitting, kicking dirt or engaging in any other physical action directed toward an official.

  Rule 3: Section 3: Article 1-l-through-q, Page 30.

Bench and Field Conduct, Rulings

• Anyone associated with a team cannot:

1. Leave the dugout during live ball for an unofficial purpose.

Rule 3: Section 3: Article 1-a, Page 29.

   a. The umpire shall issue a warning to the coach that the next offender will be ejected.

Rule 3: Section 3: Article 1-a-Penalty, Page 29.

   Author's Note: Coaches are not allowed to be out of the dugout during live ball play. By disregarding enforcement of this rule umpires are opening the door for larger problems, plus setting a bad precedent for the next umpiring crew.

2. Fake a tag without the ball.

Rule 3: Section 3: Article 1-b, Page 29.

3. Carelessly throw a bat.

Rule 3: Section 3: Article 1-c, Page 29.

4. Wear jewelry or bandanas.

Rule 3: Section 3: Article 1-d, Page 29.

5. Hit infielders' ground balls after the game begins.

Rule 3: Section 3: Article 1-e, Page 29.

   Penalty for 1 – 5: Issue a warning to the coach involved, and the next offender will be ejected.

Rule 3: Section 3: Article 3-1-a – e, Penalty, Page 29.

6. Commit any unsportsmanlike acts as follows, but not limited to:

   a. Incite or attempt to incite spectators' protests by using words or actions.

Rule 3: Section 3: Article 1-f-1, Page 29

Ruling Continued on Page 147.

b. Use (profanity, intimidation tactics, taunting, baiting or remarks reflecting unfavorably) upon any other person.

Rule 3: Section 3: Article 1-f-2, Page 29.

c. Use of language intended to intimidate.

Rule 3: Section 3: Article 1-f-3, Page 29.

d. Not exhibiting fair play.

Rule 3: Section 3: Article 1-f-4, Page 29.

e. Being in live ball territory while opponents are taking infield.

Rule 3: Section 3: Article 1-f-5, Page 29.

Penalty for 6-a – e: Umpires can verbally warn, give a written warning or eject.

Rule 3: Section 3: Article 1-Penalty, Page 30.

f. A member of the coaching staff who is not the head coach who leaves the dugout or coaching box to dispute a judgement call by an umpire.

Rule 3: Section 3: Article 1-f-6, Page 29.

Penalty: Both the head coach and the offending coach will receive a written warning to be restricted to the dugout. The umpire may eject the offender and restrict or eject the head coach when the offense is severe enough.

Rule 3: Section 3: Article 1-f-6, Page 30.

g. Confront or direct unsportsmanlike conduct at the umpires after the game.

Rule 3: Section 3: Article 1-f-7, Page 29.

Penalty: The state association sets penalty.

Rule 3: Section 3: Article 1-Penalty, Page 30.

7. Stand behind the catcher while the opposing pitcher and catcher are in their positions.

Rule 3: Section 3: Article 1-g, Page 29.

Ruling Continued on Page 148.

8. Use objects other than a stop watch, rule book, scorebook from the coach's box.

Rule 3: Section 3: Article 1-h, Page 29.

9. Be outside the dugout or bull pen and not be a batter, batter-runner, on deck batter, a base coach or a defensive player on the field.

Rule 3: Section 3: Article 1-i, Page 29.

10. Charge an umpire.

Rule 3: Section 3: Article 1-h, Page 29.

11. Use amplifiers or bullhorns to coach with.

Rule 3: Section 3: Article 1-h, Page 29.

Penalties for 7 – 10:

a. The umpire will warn the offender; the warning may be verbal or written.

b. When the offense is judged to be major, the umpire will eject.

c. When after a verbal warning and they offend a second time, it is an automatic written warning and restricted to the dugout.

d. When it is a written warning, the offender will be restricted to the dugout for the remainder of the game.

e. Once an offender has received a written warning, any further offenses are an immediate ejection.

Rule 3: Section 3: Article 1-f – k-Penalty, Page 29, 30.

Ruling Continued on Page 149.

12. Deliberately throw a bat or helmet.

> Rule 3: Section 3: Article 1-l, Page 30.

Penalty: Eject the offender.

> Rule 3: Section 3: Article 1-Penalty, Page 30.

13. Initiate malicious contact, either defense or offense.

> Rule 3: Section 3: Article 1-m, Page 30.

Penalties:

1. Offensive malicious contact the ball is immediately dead. When on the offense, he is ejected and called out unless he had already scored.

2. Defensive malicious contact the player is ejected. The offense will be ruled either safe or out and award runner's appropriate bases as when malicious contact had not happened.

> Rule 3: Section 3: Article 1-m-Penalty, Page 30.

14. Call time or use any command or act to cause a balk.

> Rule 3: Section 3: Article 1-n, Page 30.

15. Use tobacco or tobacco like products.

> Rule 3: Section 3: Article 1-o, Page 30.

16. Leave the bench during a fight or physical confrontation.

> Rule 3: Section 3: Article 1-p, Page 30.

Note: Coach attempting to stop a fight is not in violation of this rule.

> Rule 3: Section 3: Article 1-p-Penalty, Page 30.

Ruling Continued on Page 150.

17. Physical contact, spit, kick dirt or engage in any physical action directed towards the umpire.

Rule 3: Section 3: Article 1-q, Page 30.

Penalties for 13 – 16: Eject the offender. Failure to comply, game is forfeited.

Author's Notes, Verbal and Written Warnings— Ejections and Fights

I cannot emphasize enough the importance of thoroughly and completely reading, retaining and applying the rules that are in this chapter. These rules are designed to prevent and control a problem when small and manageable, before it gets out of control.

No need to take an over the top hard nose approach to interacting with players, fans or coaches. On the other hand as soon as a problem presents itself, it must be addressed. Ignoring a problem does not make it go away. A problem will always get bigger, your judgement and rulings during a game must not be ignored.

Many umpires have heard phrases such as "Don't have rabbit ears" or "Don't go picking boogers." While the intended meanings of these terms may be to help an umpire's game, they can also help lead to bigger concerns. By overlooking beginning signs of problems, you may also be ignoring bad behavior, harassment and fanning the flames for later innings.

Chirping about your strike zone, sitting on buckets out of the dugout during live ball play, multiple players or coaches out of dugout are all warning signs indicating you are allowing things to degrade unchecked.

These infractions are against the rules, the rules we umpires get paid to enforce. If you do choose to ignore the chirping and infractions, you are telling everyone it is allowed, that you are easy and will take it. You are giving the keys to the zoo to the monkeys, and you are no longer managing the game. They are.

As an umpire it's easy to get lulled into an everything-is-wonderful feeling as nothing of alarm has shown itself that day or ten games into the season. Then comes game 15 in the season, and then suddenly, it's on. Two closely competitive

Division I teams, one high octane coaching staff whose attitudes are driving their players and loud and over the top fans. Then to add to your incoming storm we have the blaring sound system between innings. This is when you since that the game is becoming out of control. This will be one of those game that has all the elements needed to test your metal and sanity as an umpire.

As the game quickly continues going south, you should set boundaries, but this is now easier said than done. The, fans, coaches and players at this point neither know nor respect your boundaries, because you have failed to set them. This takes me back to my original point, it is much easier to prevent and control a problem when small and manageable before it gets out of control.

Your first pro-active action can be as simple as a 5 second stare at the problem. Next if the problem continues, while looking directly at the problem hold up your hand towards them and loudly say "STOP". This is a great deterrent but is underutilized. Why so I'm not sure, it is extremely effective command that works curtails many problems. If your commands are still ignored and problems persist, call time and directly address the offender(s). Since you have already given them a verbal warning to stop, you can either give a written warning that confines the problem to the dugout, or you can eject.

At this point it is not about you, but rather the offender's desire to ignore your directions by continuing to show bad behavior and offend. When a coach or players have made a bad decision, it comes with consequences, and it's the umpire's job to enforce those consequences.

About the Author

After five decades of either playing, coaching, or umpiring the game of baseball, **James C. Bettencourt** decided to write a series of books called *Baseball Rules in Black and White*. While umpiring over the last two decades, James has ruled on thousands of plays. He has an umpire's perspective knowing which rules are frequently called during games. What James also knows was that just because a ruling is frequently called in a game does not mean those rules have been accurately interpreted.

For umpire James C. Bettencourt—after a lifetime of baseball, two decades of umpiring, dozens of camps, clinics, and many mentors—his own personal baseball rule knowledge and application of those rules was not acceptable to him.

So beginning in the winter of 2015, James set out to make an optimum-learning series for the most frequently called rules in the game of baseball for each specific level of play. Jim has spent many hundreds of hours researching, developing, and proofing his books. He has not done it alone; he has had help from dozens of respected and recognized umpires, assigners, and rule instructional chairs from across the country.

Jim's desire to improve his own baseball rule knowledge is what spawned Baseball Rules in Black and White. He is now sharing the benefits of Baseball Rules in Black and White so that those with the same desire can improve their baseball rule knowledge as well.